Cypherpunk Ethics

Cypherpunk Ethics explores the moral worldview of the cypherpunks, a movement that advocates the use of strong digital cryptography—or crypto, for short—to defend individual privacy and promote institutional transparency in the digital age.

Focusing on the writings of Timothy May and Julian Assange, two of the most prolific and influential cypherpunks, the book examines two competing paradigms of cypherpunk philosophy—crypto anarchy and crypto justice—and examines the implications of cypherpunk ethics for a range of contemporary moral issues, including surveillance, privacy, whistleblowing, cryptocurrencies, journalism, democracy, censorship, intellectual property, and power.

Rooted in theory but with very real applications, this volume will appeal not only to students and scholars of digital media, communication, journalism, philosophy, political science, critical data studies, sociology, and the history of technology but also to technologists and activists around the world.

Patrick D. Anderson is Assistant Professor of Philosophy in the Department of Humanities at Central State University, USA, and editor-in-chief of the WikiLeaks Bibliography.

T0352772

Routledge Focus on Digital Media and Culture

For more information about this series, please visit:
https://www.routledge.com

Cypherpunk Ethics
Radical Ethics for the Digital Age

Patrick D. Anderson

LONDON AND NEW YORK

First published 2022
by Routledge
4 Park Square, Milton Park, Abingdon, Oxon OX14 4RN

and by Routledge
605 Third Avenue, New York, NY 10158

Routledge is an imprint of the Taylor & Francis Group, an informa business

© 2022 Patrick D. Anderson

British Library Cataloguing-in-Publication Data
A catalogue record for this book is available from the British Library

Library of Congress Cataloging-in-Publication Data
A catalog record has been requested for this book

ISBN: 978-1-032-11359-3 (hbk)
ISBN: 978-1-032-11578-8 (pbk)
ISBN: 978-1-003-22053-4 (ebk)

DOI: 10.4324/9781003220534

Typeset in Times New Roman
by codeMantra

Contents

Figures

Tables

Preface

James Carey (2009) describes two things as "things to think with." The first is the work of Harold Innis. "Opening his books is like reengaging an extended conversation," Carey says, "they are not merely things to read but things to think with" (109). While this book most certainly does not equal Innis' work in terms of intellectual acuity, I have followed Innis' tendency to imbue his writings with moral urgency. Rather than deny the role my values played in the writing of this book, as so many academics do, I openly acknowledge and embrace them. Though I am invested in my subject matter, I do not think this undermines the content of the book. To borrow wisdom from the epitaph of the great C. Wright Mills, one might say that "I have tried to be objective. I do not claim to be detached." The book you are holding, then, does not provide answers; it asks questions. It does not offer solutions; it suggests paths. It does not reach conclusions; it explores possibilities. This book does not seek to understand the problems of the world; it seeks to problematize our understanding of the world. In sum, it is not a thing to think *about*; it is a thing to think *with*.

The second thing that Carey refers to as a "thing to think with" is the telegraph. As Carey explains, "the telegraph was not only a new tool of commerce but also a thing to think with, an agency for the alteration of ideas" (157). Carey convincingly demonstrates that the telegraph changed politics, culture, and economics. Cryptography—or crypto for short—has also changed the way many activists and technologists engage the world. Those people are called cypherpunks, and this book is about them and their philosophical outlook, which I call *cypherpunk ethics*. If it seems strange that technology affect human thinking, the next time you use any technology—even, say, a fork or a pencil—instead of asking *What kinds of things can I do with this technology?* You should ask *What kinds of things does this technology ask me to do?* (Ariel used a "dinglehopper" as a comb in *The Little*

Mermaid.) If you can answer this second question for the technologies you use every day, you will appreciate the ways in which technologies alter our thinking. If you can abstract from your personal milieu and ask such questions about technology at the level of the social structure more generally, you will be able to appreciate Carey's insight regarding the telegraph and the cypherpunk insight regarding crypto.

Also following Carey, the discussion in this book relies upon "a useful ethnocentrism" (2). Issues of privacy and transparency are global, and the cypherpunk movement is certainly global in scope and impact. Nevertheless, many of the topics discussed in the following pages derive from the US context. This approach results partly from my situation as an author, but it also results from the nature of the topics themselves. The cypherpunk movement originated in the US, and because the US remains the most powerful surveillance state with the most extensive reach, cypherpunks globally are compelled to respond to the threat it poses. I hope that many of my findings are applicable to other contexts. To the extent they are not, I ask that scholars more knowledgeable about those contexts extend our understanding of the cypherpunks appropriately.

This book contains no disciplinary scholarship. It is a work of what Allen Repko (2008) calls "critical interdisciplinarity," which "aims to interrogate existing structures of knowledge and education, raising questions of value and purpose," and seeks "to transform and dismantle the boundary between the literary and the political, treat cultural objects relationally, and advocate inclusion of low culture" (18). In the following pages, readers will find ideas, texts, theories, and citations from ethics, political theory, economics, history, journalism studies, communication studies, surveillance studies, literary studies, systems theory, philosophy of technology, cryptography, and mathematics, among others. I take this approach for two reasons. First, cypherpunk ethics cannot be neatly crammed into one discipline or field. The cypherpunks represent a dynamic social movement that transcends the artificial disciplinary boundaries of the academy. No successful study of the cypherpunks can take a narrow disciplinary perspective. Second, scholars across the disciplines have called for more interdisciplinary inquiry into the relationship between digital technologies and humanistic values. While I have witnessed technical scholars in mathematics, engineering, and computer science take steps to learn the philosophical and ethical side, I find very few humanities scholars who reciprocate by truly attempting to learn the technical side. In writing this book, I have tried, in a gesture of good faith, to learn more about the technical side of computer science and cryptography, and though my understanding may be incomplete or even flawed, I nevertheless hope that more humanities scholars will follow this example. If they do, we may successfully bridge the divide between technical and the humanistic.

This book is also designed to be accessible to the widest possible audiences. For that reason, I have taken care to cite sources that are easily available and accessible for all readers. I have referenced student editions of classical texts, and many of the books cited here are available to read for free through the Internet Archive. To insure against changing URLs and disappearing content, the web sources cited in this book have been referenced using the archive.today service whenever possible. Using the URLs in the References will allow you to access the archived webpage along with the original link. I hope readers will not simply take my word for it but seek out and examine the primary sources for themselves. Interested parties should visit the WikiLeaks Bibliography, where they will find further resources for studying and teaching WikiLeaks and related cypherpunk topics (wikileaksbibliography.org).

Now, if I may, a cliché: No book can account for everything relevant to the topic it covers.

Now, if I may, an analogy: In his famous routine on "stuff," comedian George Carlin (1998) observes that houses are just piles of stuff with covers on them. When you leave your house for, say, a vacation, you can't bring *all* your stuff. You can only bring some of your stuff, a *smaller version* of your stuff. Writing a book is the intellectual equivalent to leaving the house: you can't put all your stuff (ideas) into the book, so the book is, by necessity, a smaller version of your stuff. When it comes to the cypherpunks, I have a lot of ideas (all my stuff), some of which is published elsewhere (please check out this stuff), some of which I hope to publish in the future (stuff in storage), and some of which is in this book (the good stuff). In a book of this size, I could only fit some of my stuff, so I brought the stuff I knew I was *really* going to need. Perhaps a teacher somewhere will take a chapter from this book and use it in a class—an *even* smaller version of my stuff. And that's good because I know that at least they do have some of my stuff with them. This analogy works well, but there is a catch. As Carlin asks: Have you ever noticed that other people's stuff is shit and your shit is stuff? I cannot deny the implication of Carlin's question, but I can extend its logic. As you prepare to read this book, holding my shit in your hands, you do not yet know whether you will take up any of the ideas, adopting them as your own. But if you do, then at least some of my shit will have become your stuff.

Acknowledgments

The direct influence of two people made this book possible. The first is my friend John "Curry" O'Day, who rekindled my interest in technology and taught me a great deal of what I know about digital technologies. When we became officemates in graduate school, I didn't even know how the internet worked, but Curry was willing to teach me. He planted the seeds of my interest in digital technologies by patiently explaining VPNs, crypto, net neutrality, severs, surveillance, and many other topics, and he nurtured those seeds throughout our continued friendship. Without Curry's influence, I wouldn't have written this book. I am still a n00b, though, so any mistakes here are the result of my shortcomings as a student not his abilities as a teacher.

The second person is my friend Melba Vélez Ortiz, who insisted that I write my cypherpunk book *now*, not years in the future when I was "planning" to write it. She put me in contact with the right publisher, a fitting series, and a fantastic editor; she also spent countless hours just listening to me talk through ideas. Melba will claim that she didn't do anything, but she helped me work out the entire project. Much of the research here relies upon my knowledge of communication studies, almost all of which I learned from Melba in one way or another. But I am still a n00b in this area, too, which I guess makes me a Noob-Noob. Nevertheless, this project would not be what it is without her encouragement, support, and friendship.

Other people in my life have also supported me while working on this book and more generally. Rocio Alvarez has had a profound influence on my intellectual and personal development, and her friendship and intellectual camaraderie have enriched my life more that I can say. I also would not be the scholar I am today without my academic mentors—Dwayne Tunstall, Terence Hoagwood, and Tommy Curry. I thank all three of these brilliant thinkers for helping me grow as an intellectual and as a person without ever expecting me to become a mere carbon copy of themselves. Dwayne, Terence, and Tommy always respected my intellectual autonomy, letting me choose my own goals while working tirelessly to help me achieve them. Thank you to Glen Ford and Charles W. Mills for everything you both did for me personally and for the world generally; you are both missed.

I also want to thank Laurence José for giving me an opportunity to teach Ethics of Digital Culture, Alex Nesterenko for encouraging me to pursue a post-postgraduate degree in Communication, and my colleagues at Central State University for welcoming me with open arms. Thanks to Marty Wolf and Colleen Greer for inviting me to participate in the expert panel they organized as part of the Mozilla Responsible Computer Science Challenge; I learned so much from the amazing team they put together. Thank you to Suzanne Richardson and the editorial board at Routledge for believing in this project and in my ability to execute it, and thank you to two anonymous peer reviewers for their praise of the project. Thank you to Marienna Pope-Weidemann for permission to include an adapted version of her diagram of Assange's censorship pyramid. Thanks goes out to the Internet Archive for keeping information free and for enabling me to continue my research when libraries were closed during the pandemic.

I wish to thank my grandparents, parents, brothers, and all the other special people in my life not only for putting up with my BS in general but also for the patience, support, and love they have given me while writing this book and while being a human more generally. Words cannot express my appreciation.

Finally, thank you to Julian Assange, who is perhaps the most dynamic thinker of our time. When you see someone being persecuted by criminal empire controlled by vicious bastards, there's a good chance that person's work has made meaningful contributions to the realization of justice. This book represents my small part in spreading cypherpunk ideas, and I hope to one day see a world saturated with courageous people—a world with many Julians.

1 Introduction

KOKR KFQG GWQC, AQNW FICW DBKF XWDF HID.
—AQCN AKYY WC

Privacy for the Weak, Transparency for the Powerful

In September 1992, a group of approximately 20 computer activists
convened in a Berkeley-area living room to discuss their growing concerns about threats to privacy in the digital age (Levy 2001; Greenberg
2012). All who were present at the meeting understood the fundamental truth about digital communication: that it is highly susceptible to
third-party interception. When a computer in New York communicates with a computer in Los Angeles, the protocol leaves a permanent,
visible record of the connection, and the information transmitted over
the network (the content and the metadata) may be surveilled by anyone who happens to be monitoring the transmission. Concern about
surveillance was not merely a theoretical matter, for between the 1960s
and the 1990s, the US government had been involved in several surveillance scandals (Bamford 1982; Burnham 1983; Levy 2001). With
technological and political changes making mass surveillance almost
inevitable, these activists agreed that digital cryptography—the "art
and science of keeping messages secure" (Schneier 1996, 1)—was the
most important tool, the only effective tool, for preserving privacy and
free speech in a world increasingly dominated by computers and fiber
optic networks. With digital cryptography, or crypto for short, computer users would be able to encipher their communications and their
economic transactions using algorithms that not even the most powerful computers could unlock, thereby preventing government agents,
corporate spies, and other criminals from monitoring or intercepting
information sent across the newly public internet. While the group
originally considered the tongue-in-cheek title Cryptology Amateurs

DOI: 10.4324/9781003220534-1

for Social Irresponsibility, they eventually settled on a more fitting name: the cypherpunks.

In the weeks that followed their inaugural meeting, the cypherpunks created a listserv through which they could share ideas. One of the first documents to be shared on the cypherpunk listserv was "A Cypherpunk's Manifesto," written by Eric Hughes, who, with John Gilmore and Timothy C. May, cofounded the movement. In the manifesto, Hughes (2001) articulates the basic philosophical insight of the cypherpunks: that digital communication systems were, by their very nature, antithetical to privacy. Defining privacy as "the power to selectively reveal oneself," Hughes notes that computers undermine this power. "When my identity is revealed by the underlying mechanisms of the transaction," he writes, "I have no privacy. I cannot here selectively reveal myself; I must always reveal myself" (81–82). Hughes observes that "governments, corporations, and other large, faceless organizations" have no incentive to grant computer users privacy; in fact, it is in their interest that computer users have no privacy, for the more information such organizations have, the more power they wield (82). Calling for all computer users to follow the cypherpunks' lead, Hughes declares that he and the other cypherpunks "are defending our privacy with cryptography," for encryption "removes information from the public realm," restoring the power of individuals to selectively reveal themselves to the world (82–83).

Around the same time that the cypherpunks were organizing in the US, the International Subversives, a small group of underground hackers in Australia, turned the question of privacy back against the governments, corporations, and other large, faceless organizations that seemed to threaten the individual (Assange 2011; Dreyfus and Assange 2012). While the cypherpunks concentrated on the ways that the internet permitted institutions to freely access information about individuals, the International Subversives explored the ways that the internet permitted individuals to freely access information about institutions. With their newly acquired modems, the Subversives set out on nightly cyberspace adventures, finding security weaknesses in various academic, corporate, and government computer networks. Some of their targets, such as Melbourne University, were local, but these were primarily used as springboards for accessing other networks around the globe, especially networks within the US. The networks of Lockheed Martin, NASA, the Los Alamos National Laboratory, and the Pentagon's Eighth Command were all penetrated by the Subversives at one point or another (Greenberg 2012, 106). The International Subversives never stole information nor did they destroy any of the networks to which they gained access, but they learned that the world's most powerful institutions practice extreme secrecy because publics would oppose their activities if such activities came to light.

One member of the International Subversives, Julian Assange, joined the cypherpunks in the mid-1990s. Assange learned about the power of crypto to protect personal communication online, and he agreed with the other cypherpunks that encryption was a necessary means for preserving privacy and free speech in the digital age. But he also saw another use for crypto: institutional transparency. Drawing upon his previous experience seeing behind the veils of institutional power, Assange (2006) composed "Conspiracy as Governance," a short essay in which he argues that "collaborative secrecy"—or conspiracy—is "the key generative structure of bad governance" (1–2). Powerful institutions perpetuate themselves by seeking and concentrating more power, often in ways that would be opposed by adversaries. Applying this insight to modern governments, Assange argues that secrecy is the central enabling factor for all authoritarian rule. "Authoritarian regimes create forces which oppose them by pushing against a people's will to truth, love and self-realization," he writes. "Plans which assist authoritarian rule, once discovered, induce further resistance. Hence such schemes are concealed by successful authoritarian powers until resistance is futile or outweighed by the efficiencies of naked power" (2). Authoritarianism can be resisted, Assange insists, by undermining its most important tool: secrecy. To do this, Assange (2016) argues that encrypted document submission systems can be established, and potential whistleblowers—the people inside the institutions who witness unjust plans or actions—can be encouraged to leak documentary evidence of organizational wrongdoing. By using crypto, therefore, Assange concludes that it is possible to promote transparency and undermine secrecy, thus limiting the capacity of governments—and corporations—to carry out injustices.

Today, we habitually treat issues of personal privacy and issues of government and corporate transparency as largely distinct, but cypherpunks synthesize these issues, combining the original cypherpunk defense of privacy with Assange's call for transparency into a concise slogan: "privacy for the weak, transparency for the powerful" (Assange et al. 2012). For the cypherpunks, privacy and transparency are intimately connected because they both influence the overall flow of information in our modern networked society (de Zwart 2016; Anderson 2021). "The cypherpunks," Suelette Dreyfus observes, believe "in the right of the individual to personal privacy—and the responsibility of the government to be open, transparent and fully accountable to the public" (Dreyfus and Assange 2012, xii). As cypherpunk Andy Müller-Maguhn puts it, the cypherpunks aim to "use public information" and to "protect private information" (Assange et al. 2012, 141).

Cypherpunks have been criticized for holding a double standard when it comes to privacy, supposedly demanding privacy for themselves while demanding transparency for others (Brin 1998). Such criticisms, however, overlook some important distinctions and thus miss the point. For the cypherpunks, *privacy* is something that individuals and relatively powerless organizations are permitted by right and guaranteed by encryption, while *secrecy* is something that powerful organizations use to hide their nefarious, unjust, and anti-democratic plans. Likewise, *vulnerability* describes the condition of individuals when their personal data is known by others (especially without their knowledge or consent), while *transparency* describes the condition of organizations and institutions when their data is made available to publics. On the individual scale, privacy and vulnerability are inversely related, and the same holds true for transparency and secrecy on the institutional scale. Societies defined by high levels of vulnerability and secrecy will be extremely authoritarian, centralized, and unjust; societies defined by high levels of privacy and transparency will be open, decentralized, and just.

To understand the cypherpunk juxtaposition of privacy and transparency, it is also necessary to recognize that their corresponding concepts, the *weak* and the *powerful*, depend upon an analysis of power. As Huey P. Newton states, "power is the ability to define phenomena and make it act in a desired manner" (Cleaver 2006, 173), and in the digital age, power and communication define each other. In *Cybernetics*, Norbert Wiener (1961) observes that "the present time is the age of communication and control" (39). "Properly speaking," Wiener explains, "the community extends only so far as there extends effectual transmission of information" (157–158). In other words, the boundaries of a community are coextensive with the boundaries of the community's communication technology. In the small town or village, most communication is oral, which limits the extent of the community but also ensures that the means of communication cannot be dominated by any centralized authority. In the large communities of the contemporary world, however, which are bound together by global electronic communication networks, Wiener writes, "the Lords of Things as They Are protect themselves from hunger by wealth, from public opinion by privacy and anonymity, [and] from private criticism by the laws of libel and the possession of the means of communication" (160). Among these methods, Wiener notes, "the control of the means of communication is the most effective and most important," for when control over such technology becomes concentrated in the hands of a powerful few, "ruthlessness can reach its most sublime levels" (160). In the digital age, then, having power allows one to exert control over communication, and being able to exert control over communication increases one's power.

It is from within this context of power and communication that the cypherpunk slogan must be understood. As Assange (2014) states, neither privacy nor transparency is intrinsically valuable but instead must be understood within "the calculus of power." On the one hand, "the destruction of privacy widens the existing power imbalance between the ruling factions and everyone else." On the other hand, as institutions keep their affairs "secret from the powerless and to the powerful," transparency becomes a means to check such secrecy (Assange et al. 2012, 141). While the internet has been celebrated for its potential to promote democracy, literacy, and autonomy for the people of the world, James Carey (2009) notes that "modern technology invites the public to participate in a ritual of control in which fascination with technology masks the underlying factors of politics and power" (150). In Assange's words, we may be excited about "people being able to Google and search for the blogs of the world and people's comments," but we should not conclude that access to blogs is equivalent to "powerful insiders knowing every credit card transaction in the world" (Assange et al. 2012, 143). The two are not equal: they do not require equivalent degrees of power to achieve, and they do not result in equivalent augmentations of power for the respective parties. Having access to the records of all financial transactions in the world requires special, centralized corporate and governmental power, and it results in far more power than results from reading all the blogs in the world. Thus, by advocating privacy for the weak and transparency for the powerful, the cypherpunks hope to shift the balance of power, taking power from corporate and government elites and returning it to the people.

Hackers, Cyberpunks, and Cypherpunks

To understand the characteristics of the cypherpunk movement, it is necessary to note the ways in which the cypherpunks differ from two other related but ultimately distinct technology-inspired subcultures: *hackers* and *cyberpunks*. Both the hacker ethic and cyberpunk literature exerted some influence over the cypherpunks, but there are important reasons for recognizing the cypherpunks as a movement in their own right.

The hacker subculture emerged among a group of programmers in the computer labs of the Massachusetts Institute of Technology (MIT) in the 1960s; over the next two decades, it migrated to California, where the hardware and video game hackers initiated the personal computer revolution. Despite their geographical and professional differences, the hackers all seemed to share an implicit set of beliefs: that computers could improve people's lives, that access to computers ought to be unfettered, that systems of centralized authority ought to be replaced with decentralized systems, that people should take a hands-on approach to technology, and—perhaps most famously—that all information should be free. By the early 1980s, however, the hacker ethos of openness, sharing, and decentralization had been eclipsed by business imperatives, with emerging computer and software manufacturers facing financial incentives that promoted the development of a closed, proprietary, and centralized culture (Levy 2010). Meanwhile, the revolution in personal computers carried the hacker ethic out of the labs and into private homes, where an international hacker underground emerged. Like their predecessors, underground hackers—including groups like the International Subversives—believed in open, decentralized systems and the freedom of information, but unlike their predecessors, who enacted these values in computer labs isolated from the larger society, underground hackers enacted these values in direct conflict with corporate and government authority. These underground hackers scoffed at the notion that ideas could be owned, and they openly defied centralized authority by penetrating public and private networks with restricted access. The authorities, of course, viewed underground hackers not as a subculture with different values but as criminals in need of punishment. Thus, the early 1990s witnessed an international "hacker crackdown" in which police harassed, sabotaged, and arrested many accused hackers, while corporate-owned media transformed the image of a "hacker" into an existential threat to civilization (Sterling 1992; Hafner and Markoff 1995; Dreyfus and Assange 2012).

Academic accounts of the cypherpunks have, to varying degrees, overemphasized the similarities between hackers and cypherpunks, often obliterating any difference between the two (Coleman and Golub 2008; Villena Saldaña 2011; Marechal 2013; Hellegren 2017; Di Salvo 2020; Jarvis 2021). For one thing, none of the founding cypherpunks were members of the hacker underground. More importantly, the cypherpunk emphasis on cryptography and concern about privacy distinguishes them from hackers. Writing about Whitfield Diffie, one of the pioneers of public key encryption, Levy (2001) explains that "unlike some of his hacker colleagues, whose greatest kick came from playing in forbidden computer playgrounds, Diffie was drawn to questions of what software could be written to ensure that someone's files could not be accessed by intruders" (10). In fact, in the 1970s, computer scientists "knew almost nothing about cryptography" unless they worked for the National Security Agency (168). Hackers tacitly agreed that "all information should be free," but following Diffie, cypherpunks provided an important corrective to this principle, insisting on a distinction between public information, which ought to be free, and personal information, which ought to be private. While hacker culture has since come to accept the cypherpunk distinction between public and private information (Chaos Computer Club n.d.), it would nevertheless be a mistake to simply equate cypherpunk ethics with hacker ethics.

While the hackers were active on their computers, the *cyber*punk literary movement arose alongside them, articulating an image of technology-based rebellion through science fiction. As a science fiction subgenre, cyberpunk literature imagines dystopian futures defined by technological advancement and social disorder. As Thomas Michaud (2008) explains, "Cyberpunk is a science fiction movement that describes the future of industrial countries, depicting the influence of massive telecommunications networks upon the lives of individuals and societies" (65). Influential cyberpunk novels include William Gibson's *Neuromancer*, in which the protagonist is forced to navigate a dystopian society of underworld criminals, artificial intelligence, and a global network called the "matrix," and Neal Stephenson's *Snow Crash*, in which the digital and the biological are blurred and society is dominated by transnational corporations and privately owned police forces. The cyberpunk genre often combined "high-tech" worlds with "low-life" characters (Sterling 1986, xiv), most of whom represent some abstract type of anarchist or hacker anti-hero (Michaud 2008).

Just as scholars have mistakenly equated cypherpunks with hackers, scholars have tended to blur the distinctions between the cyberpunks and the cypherpunks, subsuming the latter under the title "cyberpunk activism" and arguing that "the cypherpunks were not simply reading [science fiction]; they were putting it into practice" (Milburn 2020, 377). The cypherpunks were influenced by cyberpunk novels and other genres of science fiction (May 2001a, 38); indeed, Jude Milhon coined the movement's name by replacing "cyber" with "cypher" (Levy 2001). Yet there are three important reasons not to reduce the cypherpunks' intellectual and technological contributions to mere extensions of cyberpunk science fiction. First, the intellectual genealogy of the cypherpunks has its roots not in literature but in the work of the independent cryptographers of the 1970s. Whitfield Diffie and Martin Hellman, who first published a conceptualization of public key encryption, were responding not to science fiction but technological fact. Without their discovery, the cypherpunk movement simple would have been impossible (Levy 2001). Second, there is a political and philosophical tension between cypherpunk ethics and the worlds constructed by cyberpunk authors, for many cypherpunks are anarcho-capitalists who reject the cyberpunk fear of corporate power. Timothy May (2001a), the foremost anarcho-capitalist cypherpunk, insists that "many 'cyberpunk' (not cypherpunk) fiction authors make a mistake in assuming the future world will be dominated by transnational megacorporate 'states'" (64). In May's view, corporations are just as likely as individuals to be victims of the state's ability to wield violence and coercion, and more importantly, he argues that crypto will destroy nation-state governments. Third, key cypherpunk intellectuals have found greater inspiration beyond the cyberpunk authors. For example, Julian Assange (2011, 2015) explicitly mentions George Orwell, Aleksandr Solzhenitsyn, George Jackson, John Milton, and Harold Innis as inspirations but almost never refers to cyberpunk literature. Thus, just as cypherpunk ethics ought to be distinguished from hacker ethics, the cypherpunks ought to be distinguished from cyberpunks. The cyberpunks represent only one among many influences on the cypherpunks, and it would be a mistake to overdetermine that relationship.

Toward a Cypherpunk Ethics

This book provides neither an encyclopedic overview of all things cypherpunk nor a detailed history of the cypherpunk movement and all its major participants. Other works have already provided such accounts (Levy 2001; Manne 2011; Greenberg 2012; Rid 2016; Hellegren 2017; Jarvis 2021). Instead, this book provides a philosophical look at the ethical, political, social, economic, and technological aspects of the cypherpunk worldview—the sum of which I call *cypherpunk ethics*. Given the explicitly political nature of the cypherpunk movement, it may seem intuitive to consider it a manifestation of what has been called "crypto politics," the political constitution of security, privacy, and surveillance by myriad government, corporate, and movement actors (Monsees 2020). Yet, cypherpunk philosophy is about more than the politics of security and privacy. At its roots, the cypherpunk worldview is fundamentally normative, which means it is built upon claims about what people and institutions *ought to do* and what societies *ought to be like*. Furthermore, the cypherpunks philosophize beyond mere politics, offering conceptions of human nature, theories of meta-ethics, and definitions of freedom. When the cypherpunks demand privacy for the weak and transparency for the powerful, they are calling for a fundamental reorganization of western societies—a reorganization in which governments and corporations do not and cannot track everything a person says and does, a reorganization in which individuals have unfettered access to the technology they need to bring their desires to fruition, a reorganization in which public ideas are freely shared while private information is respected. The following chapters examine some aspects of what a cypherpunk society might look like.

The first half of the book deals with the theoretical aspects of cypherpunk ethics, while the second half deals with the practical aspects. Chapter 2 presents a cypherpunk philosophy of technology, examining the conceptual, technical, and moral dimensions of digital crypto. Rather than providing an overview of cutting-edge developments in cryptography, this chapter explores the basic technical and ethical features of the technology at the heart of all contemporary digital security and privacy: public key encryption. Beginning with a discussion of crypto is essential because the cypherpunk subculture did not create the technology, but rather the technology created the conditions for the subculture to emerge (Assange 2016, 189). Furthermore, cypherpunks prefer technological over legislative solutions to social and ethical issues. As John Gilmore (1991), a founding member of the cypherpunks, puts it: "I want a guarantee—with physics and mathematics, not with laws—that we can give ourselves things like real privacy of personal communications." Thus, cypherpunks often speak of relying on the "laws of physics" rather than the "laws of man" (Assange et al. 2012). Using Ivan Illich's (2009) distinction between manipulative and convivial tools, I argue that the cypherpunks view crypto as a convivial tool.

Because the cypherpunks have never been an ideologically homogenous movement, Chapters 3 and 4 approach cypherpunk philosophy from the viewpoint of moral philosophy and political theory, focusing on two of the movement's most influential thinkers and prolific writers: Timothy C. May and Julian Assange. May has been described as "the Thomas Jefferson of the cypherpunks" (Greenberg 2012, 89), while Assange is "now one of the most prominent exponents of cypherpunk philosophy in the world" (Assange et al. 2012, 7). As Robert Manne (2011) has explained, the cypherpunk movement attracts individuals subscribing to a wide variety of political and ethical views, including anarcho-capitalist libertarians, mainstream conservatives, left-liberals, Wobblies, Marxists, and others. "The only thing they all shared," Manne notes, "was an understanding of the political significance of cryptography and the willingness to fight for privacy and unfettered freedom in cyberspace." This insight is crucial, for it allows us to see that the cypherpunk slogan "privacy for the weak, transparency for the powerful" is compatible with multiple meta-ethical and political paradigms.

The two paradigms under examination here are May's "crypto anarchy" (his term) and Assange's "crypto justice" (my term). In the chapter on cypherpunk meta-ethics, I juxtapose the moral philosophies of May and Assange to highlight the radical differences between their distinct articulations of cypherpunk philosophy. May's ethics are thoroughly libertarian, grounded in a theory of anarcho-capitalism, while Assange's ethics are a version of virtue ethics, giving priority to the virtues of justice and courage. In the chapter on cypherpunk theories of the state, I demonstrate how May's anarcho-capitalist rejection of the state and Assange's cybernetic theory of the state as a computational network offer competing understandings of government power and surveillance. Some commentators have misinterpreted Assange, claiming that because he is a cypherpunk, he must be a crypto anarchist (Manne 2011; Di Salvo 2020). As these chapters show, however, crypto anarchy and crypto justice provide radically different philosophical foundations for cypherpunk ethics, though each is compatible with the cypherpunk call for privacy and transparency.

Transitioning from the theoretical to the practical, the remaining chapters explore applied cypherpunk ethics through three notions: privacy for the weak, transparency for the powerful, and all information should be free. Chapter 5 investigates the ways in which digital crypto allows cypherpunks to implement privacy for the weak. After establishing a basic understanding of the relationship between data and surveillance, I explore some of the central cypherpunks arguments for privacy and describe a few crypto tools about which the cypherpunks are most excited. This chapter also explores the cypherpunk interest in cryptocurrencies through the structure of Bitcoin. Chapter 6 investigates the ways in which digital crypto allows cypherpunks to implement transparency for the powerful, using WikiLeaks as a paradigmatic example. After situating WikiLeaks within the cypherpunk conceptions of information markets and platforms, I explain the two primary functions of WikiLeaks: to serve as an outlet for leaks that cripple the cybernetic state and to operate a media outlet that practices scientific journalism, the practice of publishing the primary source documents that inform the journalist's reporting.

Chapter 7 turns to one of the primary continuities between the hacker ethic and cypherpunk ethics, showing how the notion that "all information should be free" permeates cypherpunk thinking. For cypherpunks as for hackers, barriers are the enemies of an open culture, which is why both movements oppose censorship and "intellectual property" regulations. Drawing on the works of Richard Stallman and Aaron Swartz, I clarify the basic ideas of the free software and open access movements and why the cypherpunks are ardent supporters of those movements.

The conclusion poses essential questions regarding the future of crypto and cypherpunk ethics for the remainder of the twenty-first century, but such questions are only possible because the future is open, because it depends on what we *do*. James Carey (2009) argues that all electronic media—from the telegraph to the internet—promote the same type of civilization: "a powerhouse society dedicated to wealth, power, and productivity, to technical perfectionism and ethical nihilism." While we might be soothed by rhetorical flourishes and lyrical upsurges, Carey insists that "only the work of politics and the day-by-day attempt to maintain another and contradictory pattern of life, thought, and scholarship" will prevent the worst (131). The cypherpunks agree. In his assessment of the internet, Assange (2014) echoes Carey, first by observing that the future is open and then in calling for concrete political action:

> the Internet is too complex to be unequivocally categorized as a "tyrannical" or a "democratic" phenomenon...[yet] It is too early to say whether the "democratizing" or the "tyrannical" side of the Internet will eventually win out. But acknowledging them—and perceiving them as the field of struggle—is the first step toward acting effectively. Humanity cannot now reject the Internet, but clearly we cannot surrender it either. Instead, we have to fight for it. Just as the dawn of atomic weapons inaugurated the Cold War, the manifold logic of the Internet is the key to understanding the approaching war for the intellectual center of our civilization.

Cheap to produce and even cheaper to spread, crypto becomes the most important tool in the fight for an open future, and cypherpunk ethics provides the intellectual basis for understanding the ethical, political, social, economic, and technological potentialities of crypto in the digital age. As Eric Hughes (2001) concludes the "Cypherpunk's Manifesto," "Let us proceed together apace. Onward" (83).

2 Crypto!

Introduction

To understand cypherpunk ethics, it is necessary to understand the technological and philosophical characteristics of crypto, especially in its digital forms. In contemporary public discourse, it is quite common to refer to crypto as "encryption," but "encryption" is just one term in the broader science of *cryptology*, the science of making and breaking ciphers. The branch of cryptology that deals with making ciphers is called *cryptography* and is practiced by *cryptographers*, and the branch that deals with breaking ciphers is called *cryptanalysis* and is practiced by *cryptanalysts*. A *cipher* or a cryptographic algorithm is a mathematical function that allows its user to transform a *plaintext* message, often written in a natural language like English or Spanish, into a *ciphertext* message, a scrambled version of the plaintext message, and vice versa. *Encryption* or enciphering is the process of rendering plaintext into ciphertext, and *decryption* or deciphering is the process of rendering ciphertext into plaintext. The job of a cryptographer is to design ciphers strong enough so unauthorized persons cannot figure out how to transform ciphertexts back into plaintext and read the messages without permission. The job of a cryptanalyst is exactly the opposite: to figure out how the cipher is designed so they can transform ciphertexts back into plaintext and read the messages without permission, usually without the sender even knowing (Schneier 1996). David Kahn (1967) has traced the origins of cryptology back to ancient civilizations, but in the twentieth century, militaries claimed a monopoly on the need to make and break ciphers. Yet today, cryptological tools are used by almost everyone, every day. While most people are only vaguely aware that they use "encryption" daily, the cypherpunks constructed their ethical and political worldview around a modern version of this ancient science.

DOI: 10.4324/9781003220534-2

Throughout the book, we will use the shorthand *crypto* to refer to the science of cryptography, the process of encryption, and cryptographic ciphers themselves. The best way to understand the relationship between cypherpunk ethics and crypto is to approach the topic through the philosophy of technology, a branch of philosophy that reflects upon the nature of technologies and the social effects of technologies. Carl Mitcham (1994) identifies two dominant traditions in the philosophy of technology: "engineering philosophy of technology" and "humanities philosophy of technology." Engineering philosophy of technology, Mitcham writes, analyzes technology "from within," orienting itself "toward an understanding of the technological way of being-in-the-world as paradigmatic for other kinds of thought and action" (39). This approach to philosophizing about technology comes mostly from engineers and other technologists seeking to theorize the world through the lens of their technical knowledge. Humanities philosophy of technology, on the other hand, refers to those attempts by "religion, poetry, and philosophy to bring non- or transtechnological perspectives to bear on interpreting the meaning of technology" (39). This approach to philosophizing about technology comes mostly from philosophers and social scientists seeking to understand technical achievements and inventions from a human-centered perspective. Mitcham argues that neither the engineering nor the humanities tradition of philosophizing about technology is complete on its own. He argues that any approach to philosophy of technology should combine the humanities tradition's emphasis on human values with the engineering tradition's appreciation for refined technical knowledge.

As a movement, the cypherpunks offer an excellent example of Mitcham's vision, for many cypherpunks are well-read scientists and engineers who bring together philosophical ideas and technical expertise. All three of the recognized founders of the cypherpunk movement were scientists. John Gilmore is a computer programmer who helped develop the protocol that makes it possible to connect devices to wireless networks. Tim May is a physicist whose discoveries helped improve the design and operation of early microchips. And Eric Hughes is a mathematician who studied cryptography (Levy 2001; Greenberg 2012). But Gilmore, May, Hughes, and many of the cypherpunks who followed also think beyond specific technical knowledge by situating such knowledge within broader frameworks of human values.

Following the cypherpunks, we must synthesize technical and philosophical knowledge to construct a compelling philosophy of crypto technology. Bruce Schneier (1996) has famously observed that cryptography is both a science and an art. Cryptography is a science because it is rooted in theoretical mathematics. But as Joshua Holden (2017) has rightly pointed out, crypto is unlike other sciences because "cryptography is about intelligent adversaries who are actively fighting over whether secrets will be revealed" (xi). From this perspective, crypto can be considered an art, specifically an art of communication. For much of its history, communication theory has primarily been concerned with realizing the dream of clear communication (Peters 1999). But cryptography is a communicative art that deliberately interferes with clarity by scrambling messages so unintended recipients may not understand the communication in question. In other words, while most communicative arts help people communicate more clearly, crypto helps people communicate *with intended recipients only*. Thinking of crypto as a communicative art also allows us to see how cypherpunk ethics offers a philosophy of technology that brings together technical expertise and human values. As John Durham Peters (1999) observes, communication theory is "consubstantial with ethics, political philosophy, and social theory" because it is concerned with "relations between self and other, self and self, and closeness and distance in social organization" (10). In this sense, crypto is both a mathematical science and an artistic practice that enables particular kinds of human relationships.

Drawing upon the research of David Kahn (1967), Bruce Schneier (1996), Simon Singh (2000), Joshua Holden (2017), and Keith Martin (2020), the first two sections below present a technical overview of basic cryptographic concepts and methods. The first section introduces the basic terminology, mathematics, and history of cryptography by examining several types of simple substitution ciphers. The second section explores the creation of public key cryptography and the mathematical operations that make it possible (Diffie and Hellman 1976; Rivest et al. 1978). After the first two sections establish the engineering side of our cypherpunk philosophy of crypto, the third and final section introduces the humanities side of this philosophy of technology. Applying the philosophical terminology presented in Ivan Illich's *Tools for Conviviality* to cypherpunk arguments about crypto, we can conclude that the cypherpunks view crypto as a convivial tool in Illich' sense of the term. In constructing a cypherpunk philosophy of technology, we can appreciate why cypherpunks say that crypto is "a perfect join between a mathematical truth and a moral necessity" (Assange 2011, 83).

A Brief Introduction to Cryptography

Discussions of cryptography often begin with a description of the communication context and its participants: Alice (Person A), Bob (Person B), and Eve (the eavesdropper). Alice and Bob want to communicate with each other without Eve being able to hear what they are saying or read what they are writing. In this case, let's say that Alice and Bob are sending handwritten letters, and Eve is trying to intercept the letters, open the envelopes, and read their contents. In this situation, Alice and Bob need to choose a cipher and create an *encryption key*. The cipher is the mathematical algorithm that generates keys, and the key is the specific letter or number pattern that Alice and Bob use to encrypt their communication. Once Alice and Bob have chosen a cipher and created an encryption key, they need to do two things. First, they must remember that anyone who has the key can decrypt their letters. While the algorithm of the cipher they chose can and often will be public, only Alice and Bob know which key they chose. Eve should be prevented from getting a copy of the key. Second, because the key needs to be kept secret, Alice and Bob need some way to share the key without Eve obtaining a copy. If Eve intercepted the key and Alice and Bob continued to write letters using that encryption key, Eve would be able to decrypt and read everything they write. Alice cannot generate an encryption key and mail it to Bob because Eve could intercept the key and make a copy; likewise, Alice cannot tell Bob the key over the phone because Eve could listen into their phone calls and write down the key. So, Alice and Bob would have to find what cryptographers call a *secure channel* to share the key. Rather than using the post office, they could have a trusted friend deliver a sealed envelope, but this still depends on trusting a third party. The most secure means of exchanging the key is for Alice and Bob to meet in person. Once they have securely exchanged the key, Alice will write Bob a letter using the key to encrypt her message, and she will mail the encrypted letter to Bob, who will use the same key to decrypt the message and read what Alice wrote. Until Eve has a copy of Alice and Bob's key, she can intercept all letters she wants, but she will be unable to read them.

Alice and Bob could choose any cipher system, but let's suppose that they choose one of the oldest and most common ciphers: a *simple substitution cipher*. In most cases, a simple substitution cipher is exactly what it sounds like: a cryptographic algorithm in which letters of the alphabet are simply replaced one at a time by a different letter of the alphabet. One of the earliest and most famous ciphers of this kind is

Table 2.1 Caesar's Shift Simple Substitution Cipher

Alphabet	A	B	C	D	E	F	G	H	I	J	K	L	M
Key	D	E	F	G	H	I	J	K	L	M	N	O	P
Alphabet	N	O	P	Q	R	S	T	U	V	W	X	Y	Z
Key	Q	R	S	T	U	V	W	X	Y	Z	A	B	C

the Caesar Cipher, named after the Roman emperor Julius Caesar. Caesar needs to communicate secretly with his generals, and he knew that the enemy sometimes captured messengers. So he used a type of simple substitution cipher known as a *shift cipher* to encrypt his communications. If enemy soldiers intercepted Caesar's messengers, they would be unable to understand what Caesar wrote. To create a Caesar Cipher using English, we need to assign each plaintext letter of the alphabet to a corresponding ciphertext letter (Table 2.1). Caesar would often encrypt his messages by shifting every letter of the alphabet three spaces to the right, with the last few letters of the alphabet wrapping back around to the first few. If the emperor wanted to tell his generals "attack at dawn," then A would be replaced by D, T would be replaced by W, C would be replaced by F, and so on until we have the message DWWDFN DW GDZQ. And to hide the word length, Caesar might break the message into four-letter blocks: DWWD FNDW GDZQ. Thus, the Caesar Cipher provides Alice and Bob an easy way to encrypt their communication.

While it may not be obvious, Caesar's shift cipher can be represented with a mathematical algorithm. In this cipher, we have plaintext letters (M), ciphertext letters (C), and a key (k). First, we must construct the equation, which is the plaintext letter plus the key equals the ciphertext, or $M + k = C$. Second, we must assign each letter a number: A becomes 1, B becomes 2, C becomes 3…all the way to Z becomes 26. Third, we must identify the key: because Caesar created his key by moving the letters three places to the right, k is 3. So, for any letter of the alphabet, $M + 3 = C$. But there is still one other piece to be solved. Let's say that Caesar wants to confirm his previous order "attack at dawn" with a simple directive, "yes." He would need to encrypt the letter Y, which is assigned the number 25. To encrypt, he would perform the operation: $25 + 3 = 28$. But we do not have a 28 in the key because there are only 26 letters in the English alphabet. So, we need to add a *modulus* number to the equation. A modulus is essentially a wraparound number; it tells us when to go back to the beginning. Just like the hands on a clock face or a repeat barline in music notation, the modulus tells us when to go back to 1. So when Caesar encrypts

Table 2.2 Caesar's Cipher in Mathematical Notation

Plaintext	M + k = C modulo 26	Ciphertext
Y	25 + 3 = 28 modulo 26	B
E	5 + 3 = 8 modulo 26	H
S	19 + 3 = 22 modulo 26	V

Y, he performs this calculation: 25 + 3 = 28 modulus 26, and since we go back to 1 after 26, "27" becomes 1, 28 becomes 2, and so on. In this case, 2 is B, and the whole message "yes" would be BHV once encrypted (Table 2.2).

The Caesar Cipher was probably clever enough to fool most of Caesar's enemies 2,000 years ago, but unfortunately for Alice and Bob, centuries of research revealed this cipher to be vulnerable to an *exhaustive key search*, also known as a *brute force attack*. This particular cipher has a *keyspace* of 26, which means it has only 26 possible keys. The first key would not be very good, since it would just be the same as the regular alphabet: A substituted for A, B for B, and so on. For the other keys, the letters would be shifted two spaces, three spaces (Caesar's favorite), four spaces, and so on up to 26 spaces. On the 27th shift, the alphabet and the key would match again—the first key. If Eve figures out that Alice and Bob are using a simple substitution cipher that shifts the alphabet some number of spaces to the right, then she knows that the keyspace is 26. Thus, she could try to guess every possible key until she gets a message that makes sense. In cryptographic terminology, the smaller the keyspace (the number of possible keys), the easier it becomes to execute a successful brute force attack (guess every possible key until you get the correct one).

Yet Alice and Bob could still use a simple substitution cipher. Instead of shifting letters some number of spaces, their cipher could rely on a *random permutation* of the alphabet. For this kind of simple substitution cipher, letters would be randomly shuffled and then paired with the regular alphabet (Table 2.3). The result is similar to the Caesar Cipher in that every plaintext letter is assigned one ciphertext letter. With this key, Caesar's plaintext message "attack at dawn" would become the ciphertext message QDDQPN QD RQSV. This permuted cipher, however, provides a much larger keyspace than shifting the letters, thereby making it more secure against brute force attacks. To find the keyspace of the shift version of the cipher, we just count up all the possible shifts, which is 26 for the English alphabet. To find the keyspace of the random permutation version of the cipher, we must

Table 2.3 A Permutation Simple Substitution Cipher

Alphabet	A	B	C	D	E	F	G	H	I	J	K	L	M
Key	Q	E	P	R	W	O	X	B	K	J	N	Y	A
Alphabet	N	O	P	Q	R	S	T	U	V	W	X	Y	Z
Key	V	H	G	L	C	F	D	I	T	S	U	Z	M

calculate a factorial of 26, which means multiplying 26 × 25 × 24 × ... and so on ... × 2 × 1. In mathematics, this factorial is expressed as 26!. For Eve to successfully break this cipher, she would have to try not just 26 keys but 403,291,461,126,605,635,584,000,000—over 403 septillion—possible keys. Even with modern computing power, it would be extremely difficult for Eve to successfully execute a brute force attack on this key. If Eve's computer can handle 100 million instructions per second, then it would take her computer approximately 127 billion years to guess all possible keys. Even if Eve's computer gets the right key after guessing only 20 percent of all keys, it would have taken over 25 billion years.

Though using a random permutation makes the encryption more secure against brute force attacks, Eve still has a few methods she can use to decrypt Alice and Bob's letters. For example, if Eve knows that Alice and Bob are communicating in English, then she can use a *letter frequency attack* to figure out the encryption key. As any veteran Scrabble player knows, not all letters in English are used at the same rate. While letters like E and T appear approximately ten-to-twelve percent of the time, letters like K and V appear only approximately one percent of the time ("English Letter Frequency" n.d.). Once Eve collects enough of Alice and Bob's letters, she can see how often each ciphertext letter appears. A letter that appears about ten percent of the time is more likely to be a T than a V. Once Eve figures out enough letters, then she can solve the puzzle like a *Wheel of Fortune* contestant and use the resulting key to read all future letters between Alice and Bob. Likewise, if Eve ever gets two copies of the same letter, one in plaintext and one in ciphertext, she could perform a *known-plaintext attack* by reverse engineering the encryption key. These methods provide Eve with an opportunity to figure out the key without waiting 127 billion years for her computer to guess every single permutation.

While there are many more cryptographic methods and many more cryptanalytic attacks to discuss, our examination of Alice and Bob using simple substitution ciphers to prevent Eve from reading their letters provides a foundation in the basic mathematical and technical principles of crypto. As we have seen, cryptography is most important when two or more people, like Alice and Bob, want to communicate without snoopers, like Eve, reading their correspondence. While Eve might know *that* Alice and Bob are exchanging letters, crypto can prevent her from knowing *what* they are saying. But Alice and Bob also had to gradually increase their communication security as Eve developed more sophisticated cryptanalytic attacks. Once they realized that Eve could easily break Caesar's shift cipher using a brute force attack, they decided to generate a new cryptographic key using random permutation. While this cryptographic method is much stronger, Eve could potentially figure out Alice and Bob's key by using letter frequency or known-plaintext attacks.

At the start of this section, we noted that Alice and Bob needed to remember two things: first, their encryption key must be kept secret; and second, they must share their key over some secure channel. Our discussion so far has dealt primarily with the first issue. Assuming Alice and Bob can meet to share an encryption key in person, we can say that they have shared the key over a secure channel. But a new problem was introduced with the invention of the telegraph, the first electronic communication medium, in the mid-nineteenth century. As James Carey (2009) observes, telegraphy "permitted for the first time the effective separation of communication and transportation" (157). Until the telegraph, letters could only travel as fast as people—on foot, on horseback, by wagon, by boat. But the telegraph separated transportation and communication, allowing the latter to travel instantaneously. Though we often forget about the telegraph today, Carey reminds us that we still live in a telegraphic age. "The separation of communication from transportation," Carey writes, "has been exploited in most subsequent developments in communication down to computer control systems" (157). In a post-telegraphy world, Alice and Bob could not take advantage of the fast means of communication *and* retain their privacy, for they still had to share an encryption key by meeting in person. Thus, electronic communication from the telegraph to the internet introduced a new problem for cryptographers: Is it possible to share encryption keys without ever meeting in person?

The Public Key Crypto Revolution

"We stand today on the brink of a revolution in cryptography," wrote Whitfield Diffie and Martin Hellman in 1976 (644). For over 2,000 years, all cryptography had been *symmetric key cryptography*, which means that both the sender who encrypts the message and the receiver who decrypts the message use the exact same key. When Caesar sent orders to his generals, they used the same key. When Alice writes a letter to Bob, they use the same key. The notion that a cryptosystem could only have one key was so established in cryptographic science that most people believed that no other method was possible. Thus, when Diffie and Hellman introduced *asymmetric key cryptography* in their 1976 paper "New Directions in Cryptography," they truly revolutionized crypto. Asymmetric key cryptography is more commonly known as *public key cryptography* because, unlike the simple substitution ciphers discussed above, this type of cryptosystem allows its users to publicly distribute the encryption key. Whereas Caesar and Alice and Bob had to keep the encryption key secret from eavesdroppers, Diffie and Hellman demonstrated that it was possible to design a cryptosystem with two keys—a public encryption key and a private decryption key. Though public key crypto would not be fully developed until Ron Rivest et al. (1978) provided a mathematical method for making it work, Diffie and Hellman truly revolutionized crypto with their public key cryptosystem.

Like symmetric key cryptosystems, we must understand the conceptual and mathematical basics of public key crypto to fully appreciate its relevance to ethical and social values. One way to understand the public key crypto revolution is to distinguish between the *key strength problem* and the *key distribution problem*. As the discussion of simple substitution ciphers reveals, the key strength problem can be solved, at least partly, by making encryption keys more mathematically complex and thus increasing the keyspace. But a large keyspace does not solve the key distribution problem, for encryption provides little security if it is impossible to share encryption keys securely. While Carey may be correct that telegraphy separated communication from transportation, we must note that the telegraph *did not* separate encryption key distribution from transportation. Though the telegraph may allow Alice and Bob to abandon handwritten letters in favor of sending telegrams, they still could not share their encryption key via telegraph. If they did, then their secret key would become exposed to others, including Eve, who could then easily decrypt their messages. The telegraph therefore made the key distribution problem more complex. Telegraphy made communication instantaneous, but private communication still required an encryption key, and encryption key security still depended upon physical transportation. For Alice and Bob to take advantage of the electronic communication revolution, they would still need to meet *at least once* to share their key securely.

Nearly 140 years after the advent of the telegraph, Diffie and Hellman (1976) observed the beginnings of the digital age, marked by a computer-based revolution in communication technology. If the telegraph made the key distribution problem more complex, Diffie and Hellman concluded that computer networks would exacerbate the problem. "The development of computer controlled communication networks," they wrote, "promises effortless and inexpensive contact between people or computers on opposite sides of the world, replacing most mail and many excursions with telecommunications" (644). Unfortunately, the promise of effortless, inexpensive communication was impeded by the key distribution problem. Sure, Alice and Bob could instantly and constantly communicate with each other—or anyone else with a computer and modem—from the other side of the world, but if they wanted to communicate privately, they needed some means of securely sharing an encryption key. Diffie and Hellman understood that the digital age posed a possible dilemma for private communication. Given the state of cryptography at the time, communication could be easy or private, but not both.

To solve the key distribution problem for the digital age, Diffie and Hellman (1976) conceived of a cryptosystem in which the cipher would produce two keys. A *public key* would be used to encrypt messages, and a *private key* would be used to decrypt messages. Alice, for example, could post her public key freely in an online directory, and Bob—or anyone else who wanted to communicate with Alice—could look up her public key and use it to encrypt messages. Once Alice received encrypted messages from Bob or anyone else, she would use her private key, which she does not and cannot share with anyone else, to decrypt the messages and read their contents. The term "public key" can be a little misleading, for public encryption key works more like a lock than a key. When Alice shares her public key in a directory, it is as if she is providing others with a lock. Bob can use that lock to secure his messages to Alice, and once the message is locked, only Alice—not even Bob himself—can unlock it. As long as Alice always keeps her private key private, she is the only one who can decrypt messages that were encrypted (locked) with her public key.

For a public key cryptosystem to be secure, Diffie and Hellman (1976) concluded that it must be made "computationally secure" using a *trapdoor one-way function*. As Diffie and Hellman explain, a computationally secure cryptosystem is one that *can* be solved by cryptanalysis but only with an extremely high cost in time and resources. In other words, a public key algorithm must be solvable because the reader must be able to decrypt messages using their private key, but the algorithm must be extremely difficult to solve for anyone without the private key. Diffie and Hellman argued that public key crypto should be built on a one-way function, a mathematical operation that is easy to perform but nearly impossible to reverse. In practice, Alice's public key would be an equation, specifically a one-way function, and Bob would use that equation to lock his messages to Alice. Because it would be nearly impossible for someone to reverse the one-way function that makes up Alice's public key, it would be very difficult (but not impossible) for Eve to break the encryption using cryptanalytic methods. However, Alice *can* decrypt messages easily because she has the trapdoor, the secret information that allows her to reverse the one-way function. As Diffie and Hellman put it, "A trap-door cipher is one which strongly resists cryptanalysis by anyone not in possession of trap-door information used in the design of the cipher" (652). Thus, a trapdoor one-way function allows the intended recipient to decrypt and read messages while preventing unintended recipients like Eve from performing successful cryptanalytic attacks.

While Diffie and Hellman suggested a few ways to mathematically create a strong public key cryptosystem, some of which are still in use today, it was Ron Rivest, Adi Shamir, and Leonard Adleman (1978) who expanded Diffie and Hellman's research and developed the mathematical basis for most public key crypto today. The cryptographic algorithm, which we can call RSA after its creators Rivest, Shamir, and Adleman, is similar to the algorithm that constitutes Caesar's shift cipher. Thus, we have plaintext letters (M), ciphertext letters (C), and a modulus number (N). Unlike the Caesar Cipher, which *adds* the plaintext M to the key k, the RSA cipher uses an exponent e to make the equation more complex and therefore more difficult to compute. The equation for the Caesar Cipher is the plaintext letter plus the key equals the ciphertext modulo 26, or $M + k = C$ *modulo 26*, but the equation for an RSA cipher is the plaintext exponentiated to e modulo N equals the ciphertext, or M^e *modulo N = C*. Using this equation, Alice picks number values for e and N and shares those numbers as her public key. When Bob is ready to send Alice a message, he exponentiates his plaintext message by Alice's chosen e and modulates it by Alice's chosen N to create the ciphertext.

Let's assume Bob sent an encrypted message to Alice but that Eve also intercepted a copy of the ciphertext. In this scenario, we can understand why Alice can decrypt the message while Eve cannot. When Bob encrypted his message, he knew the number values for e and N (Alice's public key) and for M (his message). Alice's encryption key is public, so we can assume that, like Bob, Eve knows Alice's e and N. Knowing Alice's e and N, however, does not help Eve decrypt the message because Alice's private key is not e and N but d and N. In other words, the equation making up Alice's decryption key is the ciphertext message exponentiated to d modulo N equals the plaintext message, or C^d *modulo* $N = M$. Eve knows N, but she does not know d. Alice, on the other hand, knows d and keeps it a secret from everyone, for it contains the secret trapdoor information that allows her to compute the equation and learn the number value of the plaintext message M. Only Alice will be able to determine M because only she has the key to the trapdoor.

While there are several complex mathematical properties that make the RSA cipher work, the most important one is the difficulty of *prime factorization*. A prime number is a number that can be evenly divided only by 1 and itself. For example, 4 *is not* a prime number because it is the product of both 4×1 and 2×2, while 5 *is* a prime number because it is the product of 1×5 and no other combination. Factoring is the process of finding which combinations of numbers can be multiplied to get a given number. Returning to our examples, 1, 2, and 4 are all factors of 4 because we can multiply either 4×1 or 2×2 to get 4. But 5 only has two factors, 1 and 5. Prime factorization is the process of factoring a number to determine which prime numbers are among its factors. Take 77: when we factor 77, we get either 1×77 or 7×11. While 77 is not a prime number, 7 and 11 are. Prime factorization is a one-way function: it is fairly easy to multiply two prime numbers and get a product, but it can be difficult to factor the product to get the prime numbers. The factoring process becomes increasingly difficult as the numbers get larger. For example, if we pick two 300-digit prime numbers and multiply them together to get X (roughly a 600-digit number), a computer can perform this operation in a fraction of a second. But if we give the computer the product X and ask it to find the two 300-digit primes we multiplied to get X, the computer will have difficulty completing the operation.

Given the difficulty of determining the prime factors of very large numbers, Rivest et al. (1978) incorporated large primes into their public key cipher. To create a public key, the RSA algorithm M^e *modulo* $N = C$ needs a value for N. To generate a value for N, the algorithm includes a random number generator (RNG) that generates two very large prime numbers at random. These primes are called p and q, and they are multiplied to get a modulus: $p \times q = N$. Notice that Alice shares N as part of her public key, and this is safe because N is so large that no existing computers can factor N to determine p and q. Even though Eve knows N, she cannot calculate p and q. In addition, p and q are also multiplied (along with another operation) to create d, the other part of Alice's private decryption key. Here is where it all comes together: Alice, Bob, and Eve all know the encryption equation M^e *modulo* $N = C$ and the decryption equation C^d *modulo* $N = M$. Alice, Bob, and Eve also know the numbers Alice has chosen for e and N, her public key. Thus, all three of them can use the encryption equation to encrypt a message. However, only Alice can decrypt the message because only Alice knows the value of d. Anyone who wants to determine the value of d must know the prime numbers p and q, but because Alice does not share p and q, d is difficult for anyone else to calculate. And while N is created by multiplying p and q, reversing the process is, as Diffie and Hellman (1976) put it, "computationally infeasible." It would take Eve's computer 127 billion years to guess every key in our random permutation *simple* substitution cipher, and it would take her computer almost as long to factor N and discover p and q.

Though public key crypto involves other technical and mathematical details, we can appreciate the revolutionary discoveries derived from the research of Diffie and Hellman (1976) and Rivest et al. (1978). For hundreds of years, cryptographers had worked to improve the strength of their ciphers, and cryptanalysts have worked to break them. This process resulted in increasingly stronger ciphers, but the key distribution problem remained. After the invention of the telegraph, communications could be sent instantly between people who had never met and, in many instances, would never meet in person. But private, secure, encrypted communications remained dependent upon physical transportation, for keys could not be shared securely over telegraphic networks. As Diffie and Hellman noted almost 50 years ago, modern computer networks were going to inherit the telegraphy dilemma: communications could be easy or private, but not both. As a result, they created the first public key cryptosystem, solving the key distribution problem for the age of electronic communications and making it possible for communication to be both easy and private. Once Rivest, Shamir, and Adleman proved that prime factorization could be used to secure an asymmetric cryptographic algorithm against easy cryptanalysis, the basic building blocks of privacy and security in the digital age were born.

Digital Crypto as a Convivial Tool

Following both the cypherpunks' example and Mitcham's recommendation, our philosophy of crypto technology must synthesize engineering and humanistic concerns. The previous two sections satisfy the engineering component of our philosophical understanding of crypto, and this section introduces the humanistic component that will be the focus of the rest of the book. While Tim May's philosophy of crypto anarchism and Julian Assange's philosophy of crypto justice will be explored in detail in other chapters, this section draws upon the work of Ivan Illich to highlight the ethical and social values the cypherpunks find in cryptography. Illich (2009) introduces the concept of "convivial tools," which are technologies that allow human beings to thrive and create in their local environments. The word *convivial* comes from the Latin *con-* ("with") and *vivere* ("to live"), which suggests that convivial tools are tools that help us to live with each other, to coexist. For Illich, the *vivere* in convivial does not mean simply surviving, staying alive; it means thriving together as free, interdependent individuals. As Illich makes clear, "A convivial society would be the result of social arrangements that guarantee for each member the most ample and free access to the tools of the community and limit this freedom only in favor of another member's equal freedom" (12). Using Illich's terminology, we can say that cypherpunks view crypto as a convivial tool, and that a society is more convivial if strong crypto is widely available and easy to use.

Like many philosophers of technology, Illich (2009) uses the term "tool" in a much broader way than our everyday understanding of the word, and he categorizes tools not only based on their function but also based on the social values and power relationships they promote. For Illich, tools include simple hand tools (pencils, hammers), complex machines (cars, airplanes), productive institutions (industrial factories, power plants), communication networks (cell phone towers, fiber optic cables), and even entire social institutions (public schools, healthcare facilities).

In Illich's (2009) view, these tools can be generally understood as either manipulative or convivial depending on the nature of the technology and the power relations they promote. Manipulative tools are "tools that by their very nature restrict to a very few the liberty to use them in an autonomous way" (43). From this perspective, Illich would say that any hand tool, machine, network, or institution that, by its very design, centralizes control of the tool, placing it into the hands of only a few, is manipulative. For Illich, public education is a paradigmatic manipulative tool. Though public schools were created to increase literacy rates and democratize access to knowledge, he argues that they instead provide centralized government (and increasingly, corporate) authorities the power to define the purpose and aims of education and impose those definitions on the entire public. Likewise, social media platforms stand as contemporary examples of manipulative tools. Though companies like Facebook and Twitter attract users with the promise of participation and connection, such platforms are primarily designed to generate revenue. As Shoshana

Zuboff (2019) convincingly argues in her analysis of surveillance capitalism, social media *appear* to users as neutral platforms when in fact they are designed to keep users engaged and generate more and more clicks—especially on advertisements. Social media can therefore be understood as manipulative tools not only because they are designed to literally manipulate users into clicking on advertisements but also because they are controlled and operated by a small group of democratically unaccountable corporate elites.

Unlike manipulative tools, convivial tools distribute power equitably and enable individuals to define their own creative ends. Convivial tools resist the centralization that makes tools manipulative. "Convivial tools rule out certain levels of power, compulsion, and programming," Illich (2009) explains, "which are precisely those features that now tend to make all governments look more or less alike" (16–17). For Illich, the telephone is a paradigmatic convivial tool. A telephone allows anyone to say whatever they want, to whomever they call, in the service whatever aims they set for themselves. While it is possible for eavesdroppers to listen in on phone calls (especially if the call is not encrypted), telephone companies do not secretly determine the aims of telephone users. Likewise, peer-to-peer (P2P) networks stand as contemporary examples of convivial tools. The most common P2P networks are file-sharing platforms, such as Napster and BitTorrent. P2P networks consist of at least two—but usually many more—nodes, all of which are operated by individual users and all of which are connected to all other nodes. Because a P2P network has no centralized servers through which all "clients" (users) communicate, P2P networks are distributed both in terms of technology and authority (Androutsellis-Theotokis and Spinellis 2004). Because all communication on social media must travel through a company's server rather than from one user's device directly to another's, they are not, for example, "peer-to-peer" like BitTorrent but rather "peer-to-Facebook-to-peer." Thus, P2P networks are convivial because everyone who joins the network has some say over the structure and the purpose of that network, decisions about which can be made without a centralized, controlling authority.

From the perspective of cypherpunk ethics, crypto is the quintessential convivial tool. Illich (2009) provides clear criteria for determining whether a tool is convivial. As he explains:

> Tools foster conviviality to the extent to which they can be easily used, by anybody, as often or as seldom as desired, for the accomplishment of a purpose chosen by the user. The use of such tools

by one person does not restrain another from using them equally. They do not require previous certification of the user. Their existence does not impose any obligation to use them. They allow the user to express his meaning in action.

(22)

Crypto unquestionably meets these standards, especially in its digital and public key versions. There is no obligation to use crypto, but advancements in crypto software make it easy to use by even the most non-technical person. Each person can choose when to use crypto; each person can determine their own reasons for using crypto. When one person uses crypto, they do not prevent another person from using crypto equally. People do not need to receive permission or authorization from a centralized institution to use crypto. Finally, when someone uses crypto to secure their communications, they express their meaning in action—even though eavesdroppers cannot read the contents of a ciphertext message, the very use of crypto communicates an idea: *this message is private.*

To dispel any doubt that the cypherpunks believed crypto to be convivial in Illich's sense of the term, we must turn to "A Cypherpunk's Manifesto," a foundational text of the movement written by Eric Hughes. Hughes (2001) argues that there is a contradiction between the nature of privacy and the structure of modern telecommunication systems. As Hughes defines it, privacy is "the power to selectively reveal oneself to the world" (81). Yet modern communication systems automatically reveal the identity of users when devices connect with each other. In Illich's terms, such communication systems are not, on their own, convivial because they prevent individual users from determining when and how their personal identity and personal data are shared or revealed. As Hughes writes, "When my identity is revealed by the underlying mechanisms of the transaction, I have no privacy. I cannot here selectively reveal myself; I must always reveal myself" (82). As a cypherpunk, however, Hughes concludes that crypto is convivial, for it enables individuals to defend their privacy, thereby restoring the power of individuals to selectively reveal themselves to the world. Furthermore, Hughes explains that cypherpunks not only create cryptographic software but also make their software "free to use, worldwide" (82). For the cypherpunks, sharing crypto software is not an end in itself; rather, such sharing enables the creation of a more convivial society. Hughes is quite clear that "people must come and together deploy these [crypto]systems for the common good," for "privacy extends only so far as the cooperation of one's fellows in society" (83). If modern telecommunication systems are subjected to the centralized control of governments and corporations, they become increasingly manipulative. Thus, crypto provides a technological means of decentralizing control over communication and pushing society in more convivial directions.

Conclusion

This chapter establishes a cypherpunk philosophy of technology by interpreting crypto as a convivial tool. In accordance with Mitcham's argument, this cypherpunk philosophy of technology has both an engineering side and a humanities side. The engineering side calls for us to have at least a basic technical understanding of cryptography, and we established this understanding by studying simple substitution ciphers and public key cryptosystems. To be sure, there are many more cryptographic methods, but knowing that cryptographic algorithms are built (and cracked) using various combinations of addition, exponentiation, modulus numbers, factorials, permutations, statistics, and trapdoor one-way functions like prime factorization, we can better appreciate the technical foundations of this science. More importantly, understanding how crypto works allows us to better understand and appreciate the ethical values it promotes. The humanities side of this cypherpunk philosophy of technology requires us to identify the values crypto promotes, and Illich's conception of convivial tools provides a useful way to understand the cypherpunk perspective on crypto. For much of the twentieth century, crypto was primarily available to only those scholars and generals who had the knowledge and resources to create and use complex mathematical systems. But following developments in computer technology and the publication of Diffie and Hellman's public key cryptosystem, crypto was democratized. In its digital form, crypto promotes conviviality by empowering individuals to exert greater control over how, when, and with whom they communicate. This discussion of crypto as a convivial tool, however, is just the first step in understanding cypherpunk ethics more broadly. The next two chapters expand upon the humanities side of cypherpunk philosophy of technology by examining the ethical and political philosophies of Tim May and Julian Assange, while the remaining chapters expand upon our technical understanding of crypto by exploring the practical implications of these different conceptions of cypherpunk ethics.

3 Cypherpunk Meta-Ethics

Introduction

Cypherpunks all believe that crypto has the power to change society for the better, but they do not all agree on what "for the better" means. The cypherpunks are diverse in their ethical perspectives, political ideologies, and overall value systems, and this chapter and the next highlight this intellectual diversity by exploring the very different philosophical worldviews of two leading cypherpunk intellectuals: Timothy May and Julian Assange. May is the intellectual founder of crypto anarchism, a school of cypherpunk philosophy that seeks to use crypto to promote an anarcho-capitalist way of life. Many, but certainly not all, of the early cypherpunks of the 1990s were crypto anarchists in some form, and this tradition of the cypherpunk movement continues today, especially among those who are interested in cryptocurrencies. Despite being in Australia, geographically removed from the California origins of the movement, Assange participated in the original cypherpunk mailing list for several years. Though he was somewhat unknown for the first decade of his involvement with the cypherpunks, he become recognized as a leading cypherpunk intellectual after creating WikiLeaks. Though May and Assange are both cypherpunks who champion crypto, Assange's views are, in many ways, diametrically opposed to crypto anarchist ideology. Whereas May and other crypto anarchists want to use crypto to promote anarcho-capitalist ideals, Assange is primarily interested in using crypto to promote justice. Here, I will use the terms "crypto anarchy" and "crypto justice" to elucidate the philosophical divergences between May and Assange's respective cypherpunk ethics.

While the next chapter covers the theories of the state found in May's crypto anarchism and Assange's crypto justice, this chapter explores the meta-ethical features of each school of cypherpunk ethics.

DOI: 10.4324/9781003220534-3

When we speak about "ethics," we usually have in mind what is called *normative ethics*, the branch of philosophy that identifies various principles we can use to determine whether our actions are morally permissible. *Meta-ethics*, on the other hand, is the branch of philosophy that steps back from normative claims to ask questions about the nature of morality itself. Richard T. Garner and Bernard Rosen (1967), for instance, identify three important meta-ethical issues. First, Garner and Rosen explain that meta-ethical inquiry can clarify the meaning of moral terminology, words such as "good" or "right." Second, they explain that meta-ethical analysis can establish how we come to have knowledge about morality and provide standards of justification for moral claims. Third, they observe that meta-ethical reflection seeks to determine the nature of moral claims, whether they are objective or subjective, universal or relative, and so on. These three types of questions can be called moral semantics, moral epistemology, and moral ontology. Robert J. McShea (1979) identifies a fourth possible meta-ethical issue, namely, a theory of human nature. As McShea notes, most ethical theories in western philosophy are built upon specific conceptions of human nature. If a philosopher assumes that reason is the quality of humans that sets homo sapiens apart from other species, for example, then reason will likely play a central role in that philosopher's theory of ethics. Importantly, McShea's insight about ethical theories relying on theories of human nature helps us make sense of the three meta-ethical issues identified by Garner and Rosen. Questions about the meaning of moral claims, the nature of moral claims, and our knowledge of moral claims can often be answered only if we have some idea of what the human being is. When we consider cypherpunk meta-ethics, then, we are not interested in whether they believe a certain action *is* right or wrong; rather, we are interested in the ideas about language, knowledge, and human nature that cypherpunks have in mind when they form those beliefs about what is right or wrong.

The first section below examines the meta-ethical assumptions of May's crypto anarchism, and the second section examines the meta-ethical assumptions of Assange's crypto justice. Though May and Assange are quite explicit about their respective theories of the state, they are somewhat unclear about their meta-ethics. To be sure, meta-ethics is often an esoteric intellectual enterprise engaged in only by academics who write long treatises, and both May and Assange prefer short essays and pragmatic action to long-form argument. Nevertheless, it is possible to identify some basic meta-ethical claims in their philosophies. May's philosophical perspective draws upon David Friedman's *The Machinery of Freedom*, which May (2001a, 2001c) cites approvingly in more than one text. Like Friedman, May is an anarcho-capitalist libertarian who places great value on personal liberty, which is essentially defined as negative liberty, or freedom from external control. Guided by the non-coercion principle, such libertarians argue that personal liberty is best achieved when each individual is allowed to choose what kind of life they live free of coercion from others, including governments. Because May says little about his meta-ethics, it is useful to draw upon Friedman to clarify May's perspective. Likewise, while Assange offers only slight insights into his meta-ethics, his passing statements nevertheless suggest that he has a romantic concept of human nature, which holds that humans are good by nature but corrupted by corrupt societies. Placing such importance on human character, Assange seems committed to a form of virtue ethics, the idea that ethics is about cultivating virtues, such as justice and courage, while avoiding vices such as injustice and cowardice. Thus, crypto anarchy relies upon a libertarian meta-ethics language that promotes individual freedom as the central (but not sole) value, and crypto justice incorporates a romantic theory of human nature that prizes the virtues of justice and courage.

Timothy May's Crypto Anarchy

The meta-ethical commitments in May's crypto anarchism are quite difficult to determine because he says so little about them. May (2001a, 2001c) explains that crypto anarchism is a cypherpunk version of anarcho-capitalism, a libertarian philosophy that holds that human societies would be freer and better organized if governments were abolished and all human relationships and institutions were governed by market forces alone. Such libertarian philosophies hold the non-coercion principle as their central ethical standard. According to the non-coercion principle, humans are only truly free to the extent that all their actions and decisions are undertaken without the influence or control by other people. As Friedman (2014) puts it, libertarian society is "a society in which each person is free to do as he likes with himself and his property so long as he does not use either to imitate force against others" (123). This conception of libertarianism suggests that freedom—defined as the absence of external impediments to one's actions and decisions—is perhaps the anarcho-capitalists' highest value. While these insights regarding the value of freedom and importance of the non-coercion principle are implied in May's writings, he explicitly avoids grounding these claims in a theory of human nature. May has been credited with saying that the phrase "leave me alone" is "at the root of libertarianism more so than formal theories about the nature of man" (quoted in Epstein 2018). For May, then, libertarian ethics are not grounded in a conception of human nature but are rather expressions of a commitment to the value of freedom. "My political philosophy is keep your hands off my stuff," May explains. "Out of my files, out of my office, off what I eat, drink, and smoke. If people want to overdose, c'est la vie. Schadenfreude" (quoted in Greenberg 2012, 58).

Though May is exceedingly vague about his meta-ethics, Friedman's discussions of anarcho-capitalist meta-ethics provide some clues about May's crypto anarchist meta-ethics. Like May, Friedman (2014) explicitly rejects justifications of libertarian ethics that depend on a theory of human nature (174). Also like May, Friedman emphasizes that freedom, while not the only value, is the central value of libertarian ethics, partly because it is the value that enables other values to be pursued. Friedman argues that there are as many different sets of value commitments as there are individual human beings, and he claims that "each person is best qualified to choose for himself which among a multitude of possible lives is best for him" (48). By promoting freedom, we enable each person to decide which other values they will choose to pursue. To illustrate his point, Friedman argues that the word "need" should be eliminated from politics. Many people claim that all humans "need" certain things, such as food, water, and air, but for Friedman, there is an important difference between *need* and *want*. It is true that we all *want* food, water, and air because we want to survive, biologically speaking. But to transform these *wants* into *needs* is, he argues, to artificially and unjustifiably elevate some values to the level of objectivity and universality. As Friedman writes, "the idea that there exist certain values infinitely more important than all others, things I need rather than merely want" requires us to assume that such "'needs' can be determined objectively" (47). But Friedman insists that values are neither objective nor universal. Even freedom, the central value of libertarian ethics, is not objective and universal. As Friedman explains, freedom is not an *objectively* desirable value; instead, it is merely something *most* people seem to want (196). In Friedman's anarcho-capitalist philosophy, moral values are not objective and are not the result of a universal human nature. Instead, values are subjective, and the value of freedom is only given priority because most people seem to want it and because it enables individuals to pursue their other values without being impeded by others.

Because Friedman offers an articulation of libertarian ethics that avoids theories of human nature and rejects the idea that values can be objective, he also rejects a rights-based approach to ethics in favor of the outcome-based approach of utilitarianism. As Friedman (2014) explains, many libertarians justify their ethical and political perspective by appealing to natural rights. Such arguments depend upon a theory of human nature because they presume that humans are the kinds of beings that "have" rights; such arguments also imply that some moral standards are universal and objective because they presume not only that all humans have rights but also that we can come to have certain knowledge of these rights. In Friedman's view, rights-based theories of libertarianism lead to absurd conclusions, especially if such rights are indefeasible, meaning they can never be annulled or voided in the face of extenuating circumstances. Using the example of an indefeasible right in one's property, Friedman argues that such arguments cannot withstand basic scrutiny. He offers a thought experiment: suppose that some immanent natural disaster will kill all of humanity tomorrow unless you prevent it, and the only way to prevent it is to steal an expensive piece of equipment from someone who you acknowledge is the rightful owner. "Your choice is simple," Friedman says: "violate libertarian principles by stealing something or let everyone die" (171). The problem is exacerbated, he says, when we acknowledge that rights-based claims often conflict, and the only way to settle such conflicts is to violate one right or another. For these reasons, Friedman rejects rights-based approaches to ethics. "Under some circumstances," Friedman concludes, "rights violations must be evaluated on their merits rather than rejected *a priori* on conventional libertarian natural rights grounds" (169).

While rights-based approaches to libertarian ethics seem unsatisfactory, Friedman argues that a utilitarian approach is more attractive. Utilitarianism is the ethical view that an action is morally correct only if it maximizes utility more than any other possible action; in other words, utilitarianism holds that actions are morally correct if they result in the best consequences for all affected parties. To be sure, Friedman (2014) explicitly states that he is not a philosophical utilitarian. "Although I reject utilitarianism as the ultimate standard for what should or should not happen," he writes, "I believe that utilitarian arguments...are usually the best way to defend libertarian views" (177). In other words, utilitarianism is "not true," but it is "useful" (180). Friedman argues that practical arguments are more effective than ethical arguments when it comes to convincing non-libertarians to accept libertarian views. This approach is consistent with his view that moral values are neither objective nor universal. If most people value freedom, they do so only because the consequence of freedom is the ability of each person to pursue their other values.

According to Friedman, this conception of utilitarianism is almost indistinguishable from basic economics. On the one hand, he claims that "letting people interact freely in a market...is the best known way to utilize the decentralized knowledge of the society, including the knowledge that each individual has about his own values" (175). If every individual knows best what they want, and if every individual knows best what is good for them, then non-coercive market relations enable the kind of freedom that each person needs to pursue their wants and realize their goods. On the other hand, arguing that "economics is a much better developed science than moral philosophy," Friedman states that "economics is not only a better way of persuading others" but "also a better way of figuring out what I myself am in favor of" (178). These comments suggest that, for Friedman, most people come to have knowledge of their values through a combination of intuition and trial-and-error. Just as we use our senses to reach reasonable but not certain conclusions about our physical reality, Friedman argues that we use our moral intuition to reach reasonable but not certain conclusions about moral values (298–299). To obtain knowledge of physical reality, individuals need to observe phenomena as widely as possible; to obtain knowledge of moral values, individuals need to test out various goods and determine which are "right" for them. In both utilitarianism and free market economics, then, individuals are persuaded to libertarian ethics based on the good consequences that come from freedom.

Sparse as his comments are, May's crypto anarchist meta-ethics seem consistent with much of what Friedman argues. May and freedman both reject human nature theories of libertarian ethics, and similar to Friedman, May never really speaks in terms of natural rights. In most cases, he takes a practical approach to describing the moral consequences of crypto from an anarchist perspective. As May (2001a) writes in one illustrate passage, "giving power back to people to make their own choices in life without government interference would be a good thing" (73). May's discussions of crypto often emphasize the idea that the goods of crypto, such as individual freedom, will outweigh the possible harms of crypto, such as enabling criminals to evade detection, an approach that reflects utilitarian logic. May also shares Friedman's skepticism about values being universal or objective, arguing that whether a group is perceived as "miscreants" or "heroes" depends entirely "on one's outlook" (76). Thus, much of the meta-ethical discussion found in Friedman's theory of anarcho-capitalism is consistent with the passing comments found in May's theory of anarcho-capitalism. There is, however, one important caveat.

Friedman suggests that freedom is something that most people want, but May seems to think that only a small elite truly understand and desire freedom. In some places, May (2001a) suggests that "many of us" want freedom (73). In other places, he speaks of a "clueless 95 percent," the so-called "dirt people clamoring for more handouts"; he also predicts "a massive burn-off of useless eaters," the parasitic slaves of the welfare state (quoted in Greenberg 2012, 58).

If May is correct that the libertarian disposition to proclaim "leave me alone" is not widely shared among humans, then the crypto anarchist will reject Friedman's anarcho-capitalist project of convincing non-libertarians to become libertarians, preferring instead to discover ways for libertarians to live among those who apparently celebrate their own subjection to government. Thus, May argues that crypto enables the crypto anarchist project. Crypto can be used to promote freedom by concealing one's digital communications and transactions from the watchful eyes of governments. The government cannot prevent people from accessing prohibited content or purchasing illicit products if the government cannot observe what is accessed and what is purchased.

Julian Assange's Crypto Justice

Assange, like May, often avoids explicitly discussing meta-ethical issues. In one instance, when asked why he founded WikiLeaks, Assange (2016) said:

> one can ask, 'What are your philosophical axioms for this?' And I say, 'I do not need to consider them. This is simply my temperament. And it is an axiom because it is that way.' That avoids getting into further unhelpful philosophical discussion about why I want to do something. It is enough that I do.
>
> (69)

Despite such avoidance, Assange has always been clear that *justice* is his primary motivating concern. "I have a single goal, not a very original one but a definite goal to my life," Assange (2011) explains, "which is to help in the creation of a more just society to live in. I am not for transparency all round, or even democracy all round, but I am for justice" (119). Recognizing that justice is at the heart of Assange's ethics is a necessary first step, but there are many meta-ethical approaches to conceptualizing justice. Bringing together various clues from his writings, it is reasonable to interpret Assange as a virtue ethicist with a romantic theory of human nature. As an ethical theory, virtue ethics does not offer principles designed to tell us what the right action is, but rather, it argues that we should determine which character traits make one a good person. As a perspective on human nature, romanticism generally conceives of human beings as good or innocent by nature, and it argues that humans become corrupted by decadent cultures. Though Assange rarely refers to Aristotle and Jean-Jacques Rousseau explicitly, their respective philosophies can be used to highlight the meta-ethical positions implied in Assange's writings. Combining virtue ethics and romanticism, Assange seems to believe that the natural decency of human beings deteriorates under the influence of negative social influence, and he seems to argue that justice can only be realized by maintaining one's virtue in the face of depraved social norms and structures.

Assange does not seem to provide an explicit definition for "justice," but it is possible to get a sense of his meaning by differentiating different types of justice and identifying their functions. Aristotle (1999) distinguishes between justice by law and justice by nature. Justice by law is particular to societies and legal systems, whereas justice by nature "has the same validity everywhere alike" (78). While justice by law is fulfilled through procedural correctness, justice by nature is achieved through a correct, meaningful, and substantive merit-based distribution of reward and punishment. Assange seems committed to a similar distinction. Justice by law is not true justice because law is often just an expression of power and a tool of the powerful. True justice is rather the universal standard by which we measure the moral standing of particular governments and legal systems. As Assange (2011) argues, "no state has the right to dispense justice as if it were merely a favour of power. Justice, in fact, rightly upheld, is a check on power" (242). In other words, justice can be done *by* law, but this does not mean that all law is just. While Assange suggests that justice is a virtue (114), he also suggests that the term "justice" is properly applied to societies, not merely individuals. "Cruelty and hatred live inside individuals," he explains, "but when I talk about 'injustice' I am making an observation about a political and social system" (142). Some readers of Assange will notice that he sometimes discusses rights as part of his ethical arguments (Assange 2011, 119; Assange et al. 2012, 85–86). While this is true, Assange is not necessarily committed to a rights-based ethics, for as he says, even the most basic rights exist to "underpin justice" (Assange 2011, 119). For Assange, rights are not intrinsically valuable; they are valuable because they help us realize true justice.

When Assange appeals to natural or true justice to determine whether a specific social and political system is just, he suggests that true justice is realized through retribution or the imposition of fitting punishments for those who commit unjust acts. Assange unquestionably believes that wrongdoers deserve punishment and that the innocent ought to be protected from undeserved punishment, which is why he says he enjoys both "helping people who are vulnerable" and "crushing bastards" ("WikiLeaks founder" 2010). The term *bastard* is Assange's (2011) technical term for those who commit the most heinous injustices, and for Assange, wars are among the most heinous injustices. "Modern warfare is not the white heat of technological wizardry and otherworldly precision the Pentagon would have you believe," he explains, "it's the same old mess of blood and tragedy and injustice. A drone might be able to precisely target a dwelling, but it can't check who's inside, or who just got home from school" (226). But wars are only the most egregious injustices. Aristotle (1999) says that justice is "complete virtue in relation to another" (69). Under this conception, a person upholds justice when they ensure that all people, including themselves, receive the goods due to them while not imposing harms on those who do not deserve to be harmed, and a person creates injustice when they deny others the goods they deserve and impose on others unmerited harms. The most unjust people obtain underserved goods for themselves at the expense of others, and for Assange, these vicious bastards must be punished if true justice is to prevail.

Assange conceives of justice as providing universal standards for the distribution of reward and punishment, and this conception is closely related to his theory of human nature. While it may be tempting to wonder how people come to have knowledge of justice, Assange suggests that the real question is how people come to *unlearn* what justice means. For this reason, Assange can be interpreted as holding a romantic theory of human nature. The modern romantic movement emerged in the eighteenth century, and it posited a series of oppositions: nature against culture, sentiment against judgment, youth against authority, democracy against aristocracy, and the individual against the state (Durant and Durant 1967, 887). For the romantics, human beings are born with an innate goodness or innocence, but such goodness or innocence, they said, becomes corrupted through socialization into decadent cultures. Romantics expressed "contempt for convention," warning their contemporaries not to succumb to "the accumulated vices of civilization" (Durant and Durant 1967, 888, 179). They also argued that philosophy cannot teach virtue. Instead, romantics argue that every person has "an inborn consciousness of right and wrong," which "has to be warmed with feeling if it is to engender virtue and make not a clever calculator but a good man" (Durant and Durant 1967, 889).

As "the mother of the Romantic movement" (Durant and Durant 1967, 887), Jean-Jacques Rousseau (1987) conceived of "man as a compassionate and sensitive being" (54), arguing that all humans have "an innate repugnance to seeing his fellow men suffer" (53). For Rousseau, this disposition is called *pity*, "a virtue all the more universal and all the more useful to man in that it precedes in him any kind of reflection" (53). Evil—or injustice—is not therefore a result of human nature but rather the product of culture or "civilization." While civilization may increase people's knowledge of virtue, it also makes it more difficult to be virtuous. Unlike the ancient humans who lived in a state of nature and had only the simplest of needs, Rousseau identifies "a multitude of passions which are the product of society," concluding that the civilizing process may do more harm than good (53). Most dangerously, culture destroys the natural feeling of pity, replacing it with a series of superficial, materialistic desires that drive pettiness and resentment. In sum, Rousseau and the other romantics believed that natural human virtue was too often destroyed by artificial human culture.

In a similar fashion, Assange suggests that human nature is essentially good but is often corrupted when individuals are socialized into sick cultures. Unlike Rousseau, Assange does not argue that humans emerged from a state of nature to form a social contract, but his comments about young people imply that humans begin their lives good and gradually unlearn virtue. When someone asserted during an interview that "young people aren't inherently good," Assange (2016) replied, "young people actually innately have fairly good values. Of course it's a spectrum, but they have fairly good values most of the time and they want to demonstrate them to other people" (125). Discussing his early years in the cypherpunk movement, Assange (2011) explains, "We were idealistic, of course, and young: the usual condition of people wanting to make a difference" (85). For Assange, young people generally have an innate desire to see justice realized in the world, and though they often act on this desire as young adults, they become increasingly cynical as they age. "In a modern economy," Assange notes, "it is impossible to seal oneself off from injustice" (140). Under the pressures of economic incentive, professional status, and powerful interests who threaten punishment to anyone who challenges the status quo, many people gradually abandon their commitment to justice. Of course, the bastards who commit injustices have unfortunately surrendered their natural virtue and adopted "the accumulated vices of civilization," often obsessively seeking positions of power from which they can take more for themselves at the expense of vulnerable others. Just as Rousseau believed that socialization replaced pity with pettiness, Assange argues that corrupt power structures undermine the demand for justice and replace it with complacency and even complicity.

By connecting Assange's comments about virtue, justice, and human nature, it becomes possible to understand one of the most philosophically insightful passages in his writings. Assange (2016) points out that "systematic injustice by definition is going to have to involve many people" (135), but people become involved in different capacities. Some people stand in close proximity to injustice, directly witnessing or even participating in injustice themselves. Other people, however, only indirectly witness injustice because modern communication systems broadcast injustices to entire populations—sometimes as they are happening. Assange argues that when the injustices of bad governance are combined with modern communication technology, the character of entire populations is degraded. As Assange (2006) writes:

> Every time we witness an act that we feel to be unjust and do not act we become a party to injustice. Those who are repeatedly passive in the face of injustice soon find their character corroded into servility. Most witnessed acts of injustice are associated with bad governance, since when governance is good, unanswered injustice is rare. By the progressive diminution of a people's character, the impact of reported, but unanswered injustice is far greater than it may initially seem. Modern communication states through their scale, homogeneity and excesses provide their populace with an unprecedented deluge of witnessed, but seemingly unanswerable injustices.

(1, spelling corrected)

Virtue ethicists often argue that character virtues result from habitual action: one becomes a master pianist by playing piano, and one becomes just by doing just actions (Aristotle 1999, 18–19). Assange takes this position one step further, arguing that simple inaction in response to *witnessed* injustice corrodes one's character. Though digital communication technology enables greater connection with others and the world, it also makes possible the mass disintegration of good character.

For Assange, the only way to prevent one's character from such degradation is through the cultivation of *courage*. As an enabling virtue, courage is "the intellectual mastery of fear by understanding the true risks and opportunities of the situation and keeping those things in balance" (Assange 2016, 143). A cowardly person will avoid conflict; a foolhardy person will haphazardly rush into conflict. A courageous person, however, will neither back down nor fight with reckless abandon; instead, they will study the situation systematically, acting on their knowledge in the fight for justice. As Assange's argument implies, cultivating courage and demanding justice are intimately connected. Courage enables individuals and groups to respond to injustice, but courage can only be cultivated by repeatedly responding to injustice. Importantly, Assange states that crypto can be used to alter the landscape of risk and opportunity, thereby lowering the "courage threshold" (143). Crypto disrupts existing power relations, and as a result, it allows individuals to respond to injustice with fewer risks and greater opportunity. As such, crypto provides space for individuals to not only cultivate courage but also retain and pursue their natural demand for universal justice.

Conclusion

Considering this examination of May and Assange's philosophical commitments, we see that crypto anarchy and crypto justice offer very different meta-ethical perspectives. At the outset, I identified four meta-ethical issues: moral semantics, moral epistemology, moral ontology, and theories of human nature. In terms of moral semantics, neither May nor Assange seems to prioritize the clarification of the meaning of moral language. The difference between May and Assange on the remaining meta-ethical issues, however, seems to result from their contrasting positions on human nature. On the one hand, May deliberately avoids any discussion of human nature, and while it is not clear whether he shares Friedman's intuitionist moral epistemology, May certainly agrees with Friedman on the question of moral ontology. For both anarcho-capitalists, moral values are not and cannot be universal and objective; they can only be particular and subjective. On the other hand, Assange seems to ground his meta-ethics in a romantic conception of human nature, and this has implication for his moral epistemology and his moral ontology. If humans are born with an innate disposition to value justice and only risk losing that disposition through the gradual corrosion of their character, then "knowing" justice is a matter not of learning it but of not forgetting it. Likewise, if true justice applies to all humans and provides the standard by which we evaluate existing societies, then justice must be universal. To be sure, there are additional meta-ethical questions not discussed here, but this sketch of the basic meta-ethical commitments found in May and Assange's respective philosophies is not meant to be exhaustive. The purpose of this discussion is, rather, to demonstrate that crypto anarchy and crypto justice have deep philosophical divergences despite both being versions of cypherpunk ethics.

On a final point of comparison, it is helpful to return to May's laminations regarding the "the clueless 95%" of people who remain subservient to government paternalism. In what is likely a direct reply to May, Assange writes:

> The 95% of the population which comprise the flock have never been my target and neither should they be yours; it's the 2.5% at either end of the normal that I find in my sights, one to be cherished and the other to be destroyed.
>
> (Manne 2011)

In May's crypto anarchist worldview, the primary moral conflict is between a small elite who demand libertarian freedom and the slavish masses who worship the welfare state. In Assange's crypto justice worldview, however, the primary moral conflict is between the few vicious bastards who use their power to commit heinous acts of injustice and the few virtuous individuals who draw upon their courage to fight for true justice. As we will see in the following chapter, crypto anarchy and crypto justice present quite different theories of the state, but even this brief sketch of meta-ethics requires us to accept the obvious philosophical incommensurability of crypto anarchy and crypto justice.

4 Cypherpunk Theories of the State

Introduction

In the previous chapter, we explored the meta-ethical philosophies of Timothy May and Julian Assange. In this chapter, we extend our exploration of crypto anarchy and crypto justice by looking to the political philosophy provided by each of these cypherpunk philosophies. Crypto anarchy and crypto justice each provide a *descriptive* theory of what the state *is* and a *normative* theory of what the state *ought to* be like, though they disagree about the "is" and the "ought" of government.

To best understand May and Assange's cypherpunk theories of the state, it is helpful to place them in context with the social contract theory of the state (Hobbes 1994; Locke 1980; Rousseau 1987). Social contract theory is probably the most influential theory of government in modern Anglophone philosophy, and both May's and Assange's political philosophies are, in many ways, reactions to and transformations of social contract theory. According to social contract theory, governments are formed when individuals come together in a group and agree to create an institution—government—that will create and enforce rules by which they all agree to live and abide. People agree such arrangements, the theory goes, because life is quite dangerous and inconvenient without government. One's life and property are not secure unless she expends most of her time and effort on self-defense measures, contractual agreements are not enforceable if the other party decides not to uphold their end of the bargain, and disputes are difficult to settle because there is neither an agreed-upon process nor an agreed-upon authority for deciding disputes. Thus, people form a social contract, creating a government that will enforce laws, protect life and property, and establish courts to peacefully arbitrate disputes.

DOI: 10.4324/9781003220534-4

Such government is legitimate, social contract theorists argue, because the people have consented to the government—consent of the governed is the *only* means by which government becomes legitimate. For this reason, many versions of social contract theory argue that the people have a right to abolish governments and form new ones when their current government has violated the terms of the social contract and thus lost the consent of the governed. Though social contract theorists have disagreed about the proper form of government, in contemporary western societies, social contract governments are often established by a constitution—a document that outlines the basic rules and structure of government as agreed upon by the public—and take the form of representative democracy, in which citizens periodically elect officials who make and enforce laws on the public's behalf.

As we will see below, May and Assange respond quite differently to the theory and practice of social contract government. Social contract theory offers explanations about the *form* and *legitimacy* of government—constitutional representative democracy and consent of the governed. May accepts the social contract view that governments are often established through a constitution and operate as representative democracies, but as a crypto anarchist, he argues that *no* government is legitimate, not even those governments that have obtained the "consent of the governed." Assange accepts the idea that governments are only legitimate insofar as the people have consented to the government, but as an advocate of crypto justice, he argues that any government that relies on secrecy to achieve its objectives is authoritarian and therefore illegitimate, even if it appears to take the form of representative democracy. In other words, May commits to a traditional understanding of what governments are but rejects traditional understandings of what makes those governments legitimate, while Assange commits to a traditional understanding of what makes governments legitimate but rejects traditional understandings of what governments are. Thus, crypto anarchy and crypto justice provide vastly different conceptions of the state. Crypto anarchy draws upon the political philosophy of anarcho-capitalism to argue that no governments are legitimate and that crypto is a necessary tool in the transition to a libertarian society populated by voluntary virtual communities, while crypto justice draws upon the system theory of cybernetics to argue that governments are actually computational networks that consolidate power through control of information and that crypto is a necessary tool in restoring the balance of power in favor of individuals and publics.

Crypto Anarchy and Libertarian Society

If the non-coercion principle is the central principle of crypto anarchist ethics, then in the realm of politics, crypto anarchy rejects the legitimacy of any institution that is by nature coercive. For crypto anarchists and the anarcho-capitalists from which they take their inspiration, there is but one social institution that is by nature coercive and therefore fundamentally illegitimate: government. Like his crypto anarchist meta-ethics, May's crypto anarchist theory of the state draws directly from David Friedman's anarcho-capitalism, arguing that all government is illegitimate because all government relies upon a monopoly of the use of legitimized force. Rather than being ruled by government coercion, they both argue that we should be governed solely market relations, which are by nature voluntary and free. While both May and Friedman advocate the transition from societies organized around nation-state violence to societies organized around voluntary market transactions, May modifies anarcho-capitalist philosophy by arguing that crypto can and should play a role in the transition to a libertarian society. Because the use of crypto by private individuals shifts the balance of power away from government violence and toward personal autonomy, May predicts that crypto will undermine the power of nation-states by limiting their power over identification, taxation, and communication. The result of crypto anarchy, May concludes, is the ascendency of virtual communities—completely voluntary associations residing in cyberspace. Nation-state governments will not collapse all at once, May reminds us, so crypto will enable virtual communities to exist alongside government for a time. In the end, however, May hopes that virtual communities—which, unlike governments, are consistent with the non-coercion principle—will completely replace nation-states as the basic units of social, economic, and political organization, ushering in an era of libertarian freedom.

May's basic political theory is derived, in large part, from Friedman's anarcho-capitalism (May 2001a, 2001c). Friedman (2014) argues that we can tell the difference between governments and markets because they each operate according to their own respective logics. On the one hand, he defines government as "an agency of legitimized coercion," which interferes with the rights people have to freely choose with whom they will associate economically and socially (108). Friedman recognizes that governments are not the only coercive forces in society, but he notes that government is the only coercive force that people tend to treat as legitimate. "The special characteristic that distinguishes governments from other agencies of coercion, such as ordinary criminal gangs," he writes, "is that most people treat government coercion as normal and proper. The same act that is regarded as coercive when done by a private individual is treated as legitimate if done by an agent of the government" (108). But just as there are no proper functions of criminal violence, Friedman concludes that "there are *no* proper functions of government" (18). On the other hand, Friedman defines the market as "cooperati[on] through mutual exchange in a free society" (82). Unlike the logic of government, the laws of the marketplace leave no room for coercion; in the market, all interactions are purely voluntary. Thus, Friedman concludes that human freedom would be promoted by abolishing governments and replacing them with the rule of voluntary market relationships. While governments inherently contradict the non-coercion principle, markets are inherently non-coercive, which is why Friedman forcefully concludes that "It is the government that is the enemy" (10).

Friedman's conceptions of government and market, combined with his commitment to the non-coercion principle lead him to reject minarchism, a non-anarchist libertarian theory of the state that says a minimal government is morally justifiable. Robert Nozick (1974) presents a now-famous defense of the minimalist state, arguing that

> a minimal state, limited to the narrow functions of protections against the use of force, theft, fraud, enforcement of contracts, and so on, is justified; that any more extensive state will violate persons' rights not to be forced to do certain things, and is unjustified.
>
> (ix)

In this "nightwatchman" conception of government, the only legitimate functions of government are courts (arbitration), police (law enforcement), and military (national defense). Friedman (2014) rejects Nozick's idea of a minimal state not only because it still violates the non-coercion principle but also because all those government function can be provided non-coercively through market-based functions. In an anarcho-capitalist society, Friedman argues, courts would be replaced by arbitration agencies, police would be replaced by rights enforcement agencies, and even the military could be replaced by national defense agencies. Individuals would be able to voluntarily patronize the arbitration, enforcement, and defense agencies of their own choosing, which means that all their interactions would be coercion-free. While Friedman does acknowledge that the transition to an anarcho-capitalist society will be not be free of problems, he nevertheless believes that those problems will be outweighed by the good of increased freedom for all.

Following Friedman, May argues that all governments are illegitimate and that voluntary, market-based transactions and interactions are the only legitimate and free forms of association. Applying these ideas in the historical context of late-twentieth-century US and emphasizing the role of technological change in his analysis, May (2001a) argues that the US Constitution, especially the Bill of Rights, approximates the best form of government one can have if one absolutely *must* submit to a minimalist government. But with the advent of mass surveillance capabilities, enabled by electronic and digital communication technology, May argues that the US government "has gone far beyond any conceptions the framers of the Constitution may have had" (79). "In a free society," May explains, "few personal secrets are compelled. Unfortunately, we have for too long been in a situation where governments insist that people give out their true names, their various government identification numbers, their medical situations, and so on" (60). In May's assessment, the growing use of computerized databases represents a shift toward tyrannical government. In such a surveillance society, governments require the scanning of identification cards and monitor all economic transactions made using electronic systems, such as with debit or credit cards. "Governments like to be involved in identity issues because it gives them additional control" (43), May argues, adding that "governments typically use surveillance powers to control citizens" rather than to catch criminals and terrorists, as they so often claim (81). When May's critique of the technologically enabled surveillance state is understood in the context of his anarcho-capitalist commitments, it becomes clear that he sees the US government, once a minimalist state, being transformed into "a totalitarian surveillance state" that seeks to increase its coercive power by means of knowing everything about every citizen (85).

In May's writings, one not only finds an urgency lacking in Friedman's writings but also see that he shifts the terrain of conflict from the political and economic to the technological. May (2001a) argues that western societies face a "phase change" at the beginning of the twenty-first century, for people will have to choose between two mutually exclusive forms of civilization: "a surveillance state" or "a libertarian or anarcho-capitalist state" (85). "The fundamental battle is already under way," May proclaims, "between the forces of big government and the forces of liberty and crypto anarchy" (86). Consistent with the cypherpunk preference for technological solutions over legislative solutions, May observes that, "For libertarians, strong crypto will be the means by which governments will be avoided" (78). "Governments are clearly afraid of strong cryptography in the hands of the citizenry" (47) May adds, because the anonymizing power of crypto enables individuals to participate in "fully untraceable markets" (55) and amass fortunes "beyond the reach of governments" (51). As May sees it, crypto provides a way for individuals to avoid the coercion of taxation and compelled identification; it also enables "the practical freedom to read and write what one wishes to" (May 2001c, 77). Crypto therefore "alters the conventional 'relationship topology' of the world," May (2001a) explains, "allowing diverse interactions without external governmental regulation, taxation, or interference" (44).

Like Friedman, May (2001a) acknowledges that nation-state governments are not likely to disappear any time soon, but May does argue that, in the meantime, the use of crypto allows individuals to live out an anarcho-capitalist lifestyle in cyberspace. "Crypto anarchy is the cyberspace realization of anarcho-capitalism," he explains, "transcending national boundaries and freeing individuals to consensually make the economic arrangements they wish to make" (44). While Friedman (2014) argues that libertarians can move society in the direction of anarcho-capitalism by educating publics and though "the development of alternative institutions" in the political and economic spheres (156), May (2001c) argues that crypto will push society toward anarcho-capitalism by making law enforcement and tax collection difficult, by making national boarders harder to police and secure, and by moving data around the world quickly, cheaply, and anonymously. "The implications for personal liberty are of course profound," May writes of crypto. "No longer can nation-states tell their citizen-units what they can have access to, not if these citizens can access the cyberspace world through anonymous systems" (75).

As crypto becomes widely used and governments become gradually weakened, May sees a future in which nation-states are replaced by a new form of social organization: virtual communities. As May (2001c) defines them:

> Virtual communities are the networks of individuals or groups that are not necessarily closely connected geographically. The 'virtual' is meant to imply a nonphysical linking but should not be taken to mean that these communities are any less community like than are conventional physical communities.

(66)

He observes that, with the emergence of the internet, people have begun to abandon their fidelity to geographically bound communities and increasingly identify with the cyberspace communities they voluntarily choose to join. Virtual communities ought to see crypto as a necessary tool, for it is only with crypto that such communities can make themselves opaque to outsiders and this retain their autonomy. The more transparent a virtual community, the more susceptible they are to outside influence and control. In May's (2001a) view:

> The corporation is a prime example of a virtual community, having scattered sites, private communication channels (generally inaccessible to the outside world, including governmental authorities), its own security forces and punishment systems (within limits), and its own goals and methods.
>
> (63–64)

Like other virtual communities, corporations consist of only voluntary participants and engage in only voluntary associations with other virtual communities. "There are undoubtedly many more such virtual communities than there are nation-states," May adds, "and the ties that bind them are for the most part much stronger than are chauvinistic nationalist impulses" (63). Just as Friedman seeks a future social organization grounded in market relations and consistent with the non-coercion principle, May envisions a future social setting in which virtual communities have replaced nation-states as the basic units of social, economic, and political organization. "Virtual communities are in their ascendency, displacing conventional notions of nationhood," May predicts, suggesting that virtual communities are the digital embodiment of "voluntary economic and social relationships with true freedom of association" (86).

In the end, May's crypto anarchist vision dismisses both democracy and the rule of law as coercive political frameworks, instead identifying absolute individual autonomy as the central political value. With crypto anarchy, May (2001a) writes:

> the individual becomes empowered to make his own decisions about what is right and what is wrong and to act as he wishes, to join the virtual communities he wishes to, to pay for the services he wishes, and to ignore the will of the democratic herd.
>
> (84)

For May, crypto anarchy makes possible the anarcho-capitalist's voluntary, market-based interactions, for mutually agreed-upon transactions are the only type possible in crypto anarchy. By shielding communications and transactions from democratic oversight, crypto prevents societies from unduly imposing majority rule upon individuals who deviate from that majority. Or as May puts it, "crypto anarchy basically undermines democracy: it removes behaviors and transactions from the purview of the mob" (74). Though May concedes that coercive governments will not disappear anytime soon, he nevertheless argues that the power of governments to police and tax individuals will be severely limited when individuals begin using crypto to regain their autonomy. As people trade national pride for participation in virtual communities, nation-states will become weakened and individuals will become increasingly free—socially, economically, and politically. As May concludes, while crypto anarchy does not necessarily destroy governments, it does create space for libertarian freedom in a time when even seemingly free governments are becoming totalitarian surveillance states.

Crypto Justice and the Cybernetic State

While crypto anarchy aims to destroy governments and replace them with virtual communities, crypto justice aims to undermine conspiratorial, authoritarian governments and either replace them with or transform them into just, humane governments. As Finn Brunton (2011) correctly observes, Julian Assange, the chief advocate of crypto justice, "is not the nihilistic wrecker-of-civilization fantasized by the American right (who seem to have at last found the Bond villain their impoverished understanding of the world has led them to look for)." Instead, Assange's politics is "a *cybernetic* politics," which posits that creating and maintaining "built-in, auto-correcting feedback loops" will push a society "towards transparent institutions and accurate information, because the cost of conspiratorial secrecy is pushed disproportionately high" (15). Whereas May derives both his meta-ethics and his political theory from the same source, namely, anarcho-capitalism, Assange shares his meta-ethics with virtue ethics and the romantic tradition but draws upon cybernetics and communication studies for his political theory. If one of the primary meta-ethical insights of crypto justice is that unjust societies tend to destroy the virtue of justice that is part of humanity's inherently good nature, then the political theory of crypto justice diagnoses the institutions of power in an unjust society through a cybernetic theory of the state. This theory accepts the social contract view that governments are only legitimate if their constituents have freely consented to their rule; however, this theory rejects the social contract view that the mere existence of a constitution and elections makes a state legitimate. Instead, Assange's cybernetic political theory views governments—and as we will see, corporations and empires—as computational information networks, which can either be open and therefore just or secretive and therefore authoritarian. Assange argues that crypto is *the* essential tool in resisting, transforming, and replacing authoritarian government because crypto enables individuals and groups to regain control over information flows and thereby undermine modern states' monopoly on the collection and circulation of information.

Assange's political theory begins with an interpretation of social contract theory grounded in the view that information is power. According to Assange (2011), a government is only legitimate if the people it governs have consented to its existence, just as social contract theory claims. But Assange departs from traditional western political theory by rejecting the idea that the existence of a constitution and periodic elections constitutes meaningful consent. Instead, he argues that consent is enabled by access to relevant and essential information. In other words, consent is epistemic not procedural. As modern western governments have become more secretive, they have become increasingly illegitimate. As Assange writes:

> Many modern states forget that they were founded on the principles of the Enlightenment, that knowledge is the guarantor of liberty, and that no state as the right to dispense justice as if it were merely a favour of power.
>
> (242)

Assange posits an inverse relationship between government secrecy and government legitimacy: the more secretive a government is, the less legitimate it is. As the philosopher John Stuart Mill (1873) once asked, in the same spirit, "without publicity, how could [the public] either check or encourage what they are not permitted to see?" (42). On this view, if publics lack knowledge of what their governments do behind closed doors, they have been deprived of the opportunity to consent. "Information sets us free," Assange (2011) therefore concludes, "and it does so by allowing us to question the actions of those who would sooner we had no means to question them, no right to reply" (243).

To analyze the legitimacy or illegitimacy of contemporary government, Assange (2006) insists that we must understand how "modern communication states" control the circulation of information to their own benefit, a process he calls "conspiracy" (1). As Assange defines it, a *conspiracy* exists when the members of an institution "make secret plans to jointly commit a harmful act" (1), and he argues that conspiracy is not an authoritarian aberration of government but "the primary planning methodology behind maintaining of strengthening authoritarian power" (2). Just as the US government hires mathematicians to understand terrorist organizations as connected graphs (see Amoore and De Goede 2005), Assange applies the connected graphs model to governments, arguing that this methodology makes it possible to understand that governments are information-processing networks that use secrecy to achieve their ends. To illustrate this approach, Assange (2006) provides the following visualization:

> First take some nails ('conspirators') and hammer them into a board at random. Then take twine ('communication') and loop it from nail to nail without breaking [it]. Call the twine connecting two nails a *link*...Imagine a thick heavy cord between some nails and fine light thread between others. Call the importance, thickness or heaviness of a link its *weight*. Between conspirators that never communicate the weight is zero.
>
> (2–3, emphasis added)

While the extent and the shape of a conspiratorial network will change from government to government, Assange argues that this basic model can be applied to all states—whether the Communist government of China or the "liberal democratic" government of the US—to understand the degrees of secrecy used and, therefore, the extent of legitimacy rightfully claimed.

Just as a computer network functions through the input and output of information, communication states function by collecting, processing, and outputting information and actions. Norbert Wiener (1961), the father of cybernetics observes, "any organism is held together...by the possession of means for the acquisition, use, retention, and transmission of information" (161). Assange (2006) applies a similar insight to modern western governments:

> Conspiracies take information about the world in which they operate (the conspiratorial environment), pass [it] through the conspirators and then act on the result. We can see conspiracies as a type of device that has inputs (information about the environment), a computational network (the conspirators and their links to each other) and outputs (actions intending to change or maintain the environment).
>
> (3)

Once we understand that a government is essentially an information-processing network, Assange believes that we gain clarity about the nature of contemporary political systems. For example, some defenders of democratic government believe that mass surveillance—the act of monitoring and recording the activity and communications of entire regional, national, and global populations—is an aberration that can be corrected through legislative reforms. But Assange's cybernetic theory of the state emphasizes the fact that governments cannot function effectively or efficiently without total information awareness of their environment; thus, mass surveillance is an integral component of the modern computational state.

Furthermore, the cybernetic state model is not bound by traditional nation-state geographies, which is why Assange draws upon the work of Harold Innis to argue that it is not only nation-state governments but imperial governments that operate as computational networks. As one of the founding intellectuals of communication studies, Innis (2008) argues that all communication media have an inherent "bias" toward either time or space, the former enabling temporal duration and the latter enabling geographic extension of any given society. Ancient empires, Innis (2007) explains, that wrote on stone could last for millennia because stone is so durable; however, such empires could not expand quickly because stone is a difficult medium to transport. As more mobile communication media, such as papyrus, appeared, empires could more efficiently expand geographically, but in doing so, they sacrificed duration. In the modern world, Innis notes that western empires, especially the US, have achieved unprecedented geographical extension using electronic communication media—telegraph, telephone, radio, television, and (by extension) the internet. In doing so, they have sacrificed temporal durability, rendering themselves vulnerable to the forces of instability. Unlike ancient empires, which sought to balance space-biased media with time-biased media, modern empires like the US rely upon bureaucracy and violence to achieve stability and temporal duration. As Innis (2008) puts it in his commentary on the US empire, a combination of "endless administrative activity" (130) and "organized force" (189) are used to achieve stability where communication media have failed to do so.

Extending Innis' mid-twentieth-century analysis into to the digital age, Assange (2015) observes that the US, "the world's sole remaining 'empire'" (3), has not only capitalized on digital media to enable its geographic extension but also resorted to bureaucracy and violence to ensure its temporal duration. Distilling Innis' central insight, Assange writes that "The structured attempt at managing an extended cultural and economic system using communications is the hallmark of empire" (3). Just as Innis observed that space-biased media make possible geographically extensive empires, Assange (2006) observes that "Literacy and the communications revolution have empowered conspirators with new means to conspire, increasing the speed of accuracy of their interactions and thereby the maximum size a conspiracy may achieve before it breaks down" (5). Digital communication networks enable the US government to link the ambassadors in its embassies with the agents in its Central Intelligence Agency (CIA) offices and the analysts in its National Security Agency (NSA) outposts to form an efficient, global communication network. Even though the US has used communication networks to achieve geographical extension, it resorts to bureaucracy and violence to achieve temporal stability. As Assange (2015) notes, the US uses surveillance and data analytics to "integrate the streams of intelligence coming in" and a militarized bureaucracy to "swiftly project its resulting decisions outward" (3). On this view, it is no coincidence that the US controls not only the global structure of the internet (Greenwald 2014) but also the most expensive and expansive network of military bases and weapons in human history (Vine 2015). In the language of Innis, the communication media of the US empire are space-biased, and rather than supplement those media with time-biased media, the US has supplemented them with enormous institutions of violence.

Importantly, Assange extends his analysis of computational networks beyond nation-states and empire states, applying it to corporations as well. As Assange (2016) unequivocally explains, "I don't see a difference between government and big corporations and small corporations. This is all one continuum; these are all systems that are trying to get as much power as possible" (132–133). Just like governments, corporations take in data about their environment, process it, and then output the next action of the institution. But Assange is quick to remind us that the distinction between governments and corporations, while useful in theory, becomes problematic when applied to real-life contexts because governments and corporations are increasingly networked together. Again, the US provides a compelling example. On the one hand, governments serve corporations in many ways, one of which is the practice of economic espionage or spying on foreign corporations so American corporations can gain an information advantage (Assange et al. 2012). On the other hand, the big tech firms of Silicon Valley—most notably Google, Facebook, and Twitter—act as extensions of government surveillance agencies by tracking all of their users' data and then sharing that data with agencies like the

NSA (Greenwald 2014; Assange 2014). As Assange (2016) notes, such relationships are not incidental, for even Google's former CEO, Eric Schmidt, co-authored a book with a former State Department advisor, arguing, as Assange put it, that "the tech industry could be a powerful agent of American foreign policy" (53). Assange explains that Schmidt's book unabashedly claims that Google could help the US government not only spy on entire foreign populations but also replace uncooperative foreign governments with more friendly heads of state. Assange concludes that the line between the public and private sector has blurred, and that corporations—especially big tech firms—are in many ways extensions of the conspiratorial computational network.

Just as Tim May argues that western populations now face a future defined by either crypto anarchy and totalitarianism, Assange argues that global populations now face a future defined by either crypto justice or a "transnational surveillance dystopia" (Assange et al. 2012, 5). Because the US government can surveil everyone on the planet to impose its will through perpetual military action, to select the leaders of foreign governments, and to draw upon the power of Silicon Valley to achieve all these aims, Assange argues that the world faces the development of

> a transnational surveillance state, drone-riddled, the networked neo-feudalism of the transnational elite—not in a classical sense, but a complex multi-party interaction that has come about as a result of various elites in their own national countries lifting up together, off their respective population bases, and merging. All communications will be surveilled, permanently recorded, permanently tracked, each individual in all their interactions permanently identified as that individual to this new Establishment, from birth to death...This system will also coincide with a drones arms race that will eliminate clearly defined borders as we know them, since such borders are produced by the contestation of physical lines, resulting in a state of perpetual war as the winning influence-networks start to shake down the world for concessions. And alongside this people are going to just be buried under the impossible math of bureaucracy.
>
> (Assange et al. 2012, 158)

Though ominous, this future is not inevitable, Assange (2006) argues because the use of crypto allows individuals and publics to resist the development of a transnational surveillance dystopia and achieve crypto justice on the domestic and international levels. Observing that

"an authoritarian conspiracy that cannot think is powerless to preserve itself against the opponents it induces" (5), Assange's call for
crypto justice relies upon crypto carry out two kinds of attacks on
the "conspiratorial cognitive ability" of cybernetic states: *blinding* and
throttling (5). On the one hand, Assange argues that crypto can be used
to blind a conspiracy by undermining its ability to gather data about
its environment. Or as Assange puts it, crypto enables activists to blind
a conspiracy "by distorting or restricting the information available to
it" (5). Because encrypted communication and transaction networks
are impervious to surveillance, both citizens and foreign nationals can
use crypto to undermine the ability of an authoritarian government
to monitor and record their activities. If a cybernetic state cannot determine, through mass surveillance or similar information-gathering
methods, what other actors in its environment are doing, thinking,
and planning, then it can neither know nor anticipate their actions.
Thus, the conspiratorial network will be unable to act efficiently and
effectively, if at all. The same principle holds true on the international
level. As Assange (2013) writes:

> Cryptography can protect not just the civil liberties and rights of
> individuals, but the sovereignty and independence of whole coun-
> tries, solidarity between groups with common cause, and the pro-
> ject of global emancipation. It can be used to fight not just the
> tyranny of the state over the individual but the tyranny of the em-
> pire over smaller states.

Not only can the citizens of the US use crypto to defend against their
own government's surveillance, weaker states of the global south that
continue to be coerced and controlled by the US empire can use crypto
to defend themselves against imperial aggression.

In addition to using crypto to blind a conspiracy, Assange (2006)
says that it is also possible to throttle a conspiracy using crypto. By
"throttling," Assange means "constricting (reducing the weight of)
those high weight links which bridge regions of equal total conspiratorial power" (4). In other words, a cybernetic state is throttled—namely,
its communication speed is slowed—when its internal communication channels are impeded or ineffective. Because only insiders to the
conspiracy have the means to throttle its internal communications,
Assange insists that those insiders must be compelled to do so, and
the best way to compel them to throttle their own communication
network is by "fomenting a worldwide movement of mass leaking"
(quoted in Greenberg 2012, 131). Of course, all digital communication

leaves a trail, including the transmission of leaked documents. But if those insiders who witness acts and plans of injustice leak the documents anonymously through encrypted channels, then it becomes increasingly difficult for other participants in the conspiracy to discover where the leaks are coming from. As Brunton (2011) helpfully explains:

> If anyone in the conspiracy leaks, and the information is disclosed anonymously, everyone in the graph becomes suspect, if not for leaking then for negligent security. You don't need to neutralize key nodes [in the network] if they stop talking to each other, or if their conversations are so restricted by the possibility of disclosure that their links become far less important.
>
> (14)

Returning to the visual example of nails and twine on a board, leaking documents does something that stealing documents does not: it forces the conspiracy to start cutting its own links, "thereby making itself dumber and slower and smaller" (Bady 2010). Anonymous leaks reduce levels of trust within the conspiracy, and conspirators are less likely to communicate with each other if they are less likely to trust each other.

In the end, Assange's call for crypto justice entails the use of crypto to thwart government and corporate mass surveillance and to provide anonymous channels for those who would leak documents from inside the conspiracy. The aim of crypto justice is not the destruction of government as such but the promotion of just government. In the modern west, governments and corporations have become more secretive about their own actions while simultaneously demanding more vulnerability on the actions of others. All governments increasingly spy on their own citizens, and empires increasingly spy on *everyone*—from their own citizens to entire foreign populations. Assange argues that once we understand these governments, empires, and corporations as computational networks that process data about their environments and output actions to preserve and increase their power, crypto becomes the most important tool for challenging existing power relations. On the one hand, individuals can use crypto to evade mass surveillance, and states of the global south can use crypto to resist the donation of empires like the US. On the other hand, creating anonymous channels for documents leaks will make it possible for insiders to reveal the unjust activities of conspiratorial networks, thereby undermining the functioning of those networks. Importantly, as leaked documents become increasingly available, publics have a renewed opportunity to decide whether they consent to their governments and therefore a fresh opportunity to determine whether their governments are truly legitimate and truly just.

Conclusion

May's crypto anarchy and Assange's crypto justice thus present differing theories of the state, each responding to social contract theory and informed by their respective meta-ethical perspectives. As the leading advocate of crypto anarchy, May argues that all governments are illegitimate because they all violate the non-coercion principle. Democracy is no more desirable than dictatorship: the latter relies upon the tyranny of one while the former relies upon the tyranny of the majority. Drawing on Friedman's anarcho-capitalism, May concludes that only market arrangements uphold the non-coercion principle because all market arrangements are strictly voluntary. In May's view, crypto represents a technological solution to the problem of government authority, for it makes the communications and transactions of individuals entirely opaque to national security, law enforcement, and tax collection agencies. He celebrates the emergence of virtual communities as sites of voluntary participation and association, and though he acknowledges that the process may be slow, he predicts a future scenario in which freely organized virtual communities have replaced arbitrary and coercive nation-states.

As the leading theorist of crypto justice, Assange argues that governments are legitimate when publics have consented to them, but he insists that publics must have full and ongoing knowledge of government activities for such consent to be meaningful. Drawing upon cybernetics and Innis' communication theory, Assange concludes that we must study governments as computational networks that process information and execute actions. Such cybernetic governments aim for total information awareness on both domestic and international scales, with secretive networks including not only public–private cooperation but also imperial domination of smaller, weaker states by larger, more powerful states—especially the US. In Assange's view, crypto represents a technological solution to the problem of government and corporate secrecy, for it allows insiders to leak massive amounts of data about harmful policies and plans, providing publics with more complete knowledge of public and private institutions. Though Assange does not necessarily foresee any future time in which humanity will have achieved perfect justice at the global scale, he celebrates the fact that crypto makes possible the pursuit of justice and the mitigation of imperialism.

Though crypto anarchy and crypto justice present to very different versions of cypherpunk ethics, they both view crypto as a convivial tool, albeit in their own distinctive ways. For May, the conviviality of crypto lies in its ability to limit coercive power while promoting voluntary association, pushing society in libertarian directions. For Assange, the conviviality of crypto lies in its ability to undermine government and corporate secrecy, thereby promoting policies and actions that are just rather than unjust. Though they disagree about the ideal state of society, they agree that crypto is an indispensable tool for achieving such states.

Likewise, crypto anarchy and crypto justice are both compatible with the cypherpunk principle "privacy for the weak, transparency for the powerful"—but again, in very different ways. Crypto anarchy values privacy for the weak because it empowers the individual to resist government coercion, while it views transparency for the powerful as an incidental fact of encrypted networks. Crypto justice, on the other hand, values transparency for the powerful because it disrupts conspiratorial institutions from inflicting harm on entire populations, while it views privacy for the weak as a complementary means of empowering publics against authoritarian governments, imperial states, and greedy corporations. Thus, as we will see in the remaining chapters, crypto anarchy and crypto justice provide us with two very different conceptions of "privacy for the weak, transparency for the powerful."

5 Privacy for the Weak

Introduction

When it comes to naming our contemporary world, we often rotate between three different terms: the digital age, the information age, and the surveillance age. Each of these titles is accurate but partial, for each one captures one of three interrelated characteristics of the early twentieth century. The "digital" age refers to the twentieth-century revolution in digital computing and telecommunication networks. The "information" age refers to the fact that the digital computing revolution accelerated our ability to create, store, share, access, and modify information (Webster 2006). The "surveillance" age refers to the development of government and corporate mass surveillance systems designed to monitor, extract, record, sort, analyze, and exploit the information created with digital technologies (Greenwald 2014; Zuboff 2019).

From a cypherpunk perspective, we should approach this digital-information-surveillance age with caution, for it brings great promise and grave threats. Cypherpunks embrace the digital revolution and champion computers and crypto as convivial tools; they also embrace the increase in information and communication made possible by the digital revolution. However, they fear the rise of "transnational surveillance dystopias" in which "all communications will be surveilled, permanently recorded, permanently tracked, each individual in all their interactions permanently identified as that individual... from birth to death" (Assange et al. 2012, 5, 158). The cypherpunk opposition to mass surveillance is not the result of conspiracy-minded musings but the refection of an accurate understanding of our time. Government agencies and corporations want to collect all the data, all the time—and they now use sophisticated surveillance systems to accomplish this goal. Most concerning is the fact that mass surveillance

DOI: 10.4324/9781003220534-5

is only possible because government agencies and corporations often work together (Bamford 1982, 2008; Greenwald 2014). Against the emergence of mass surveillance dystopias, the cypherpunks apply the first half of their guiding slogan: *privacy for the weak, transparency for the powerful.*

As a movement interested contesting the power distribution in twenty-first-century societies, the cypherpunks argue that we must use crypto to defend our privacy and that we must use our privacy as a means of empowering individuals and relatively powerless organizations. Governments and corporations seek total information awareness regarding the behavior of individuals and publics worldwide because such knowledge increases their power. As Julian Assange (2011) writes, "Regimes often rely on having control of the data, and they can hurt people or oppress them or silence them by means of such control" (79). Cypherpunks argue that voting will not and cannot bring an end to mass surveillance because governments—especially western governments—are the primacy culprits of mass surveillance. Thus, they urge individuals and groups to learn to use crypto for information self-defense. As Assange concludes, "the only effective defense against the coming surveillance dystopia is one where you take steps yourself to safeguard your privacy, because there's no incentive for self-restraint by the people that have the capacity to intercept everything" (Assange et al. 2012, 62). Thinking beyond mere privacy, Tim May (2001b) argues that crypto will make "totally anonymous" and "untraceable" personal communications and economic transactions possible (62). Though May's crypto anarchy and Assange's crypto justice envision two very different worlds emerging from the spread of crypto, they largely agree that real, crypto-enabled privacy for the weak is a necessary part of digital age politics.

In the sections that follow, we will explore the cypherpunk notion "privacy for the weak" within the contemporary information and surveillance context. Jacob Appelbaum explains that one key cypherpunk insight is that "the architecture actually defines the political situation," which means that we must understand how data, surveillance, and crypto work in context before we reach ethical conclusions about them (Assange et al. 2012, 88). The first section introduces the basic terminology for understanding various states of data, different forms of surveillance, and the relevant uses of crypto. The second section explores various cypherpunk arguments surveillance and privacy. May's crypto anarchy and Assange's crypto justice are relevant perspectives here, but other cypherpunk voices are also introduced to broaden our understanding of "privacy for the weak." Transitioning away from information and communication to economic transactions, the third section introduces the cypherpunk perspective on the use of crypto-currencies as another means to privacy for the weak. Though there are many cryptocurrencies, the discussion here will use Bitcoin as a representative example in order to illustrate the cypherpunk call for anonymous, stateless crypto cash. Though true anonymity is still impossible, cypherpunks advocate a wide variety of crypto tools in their defense of privacy for the weak.

Data, Surveillance, Crypto

To appreciate the various ways that cypherpunk ethics can be used to understand and pursue "privacy for the weak," we must understand how data, surveillance, and crypto relate to each other within the contemporary technological context (Assange et al. 2012). For the present discussion, *data* can be defined as any information, files, messages, media, or any other content that is created, shared, and saved on digital and telecommunication devices. Such data exist in two basic states. When data is saved on a drive somewhere—whether this be the hard drive of your personal device, an external hard drive or USB flash drive, or a cloud server owned and operated by a large tech firm—it is considered *data-at-rest*. When data is being sent from one device to another over a network of any size, it is considered *data-in-transit*. These two categories are considered two *states* of data and not two different types of data because any individual digital data object can be saved to a drive, and thus be "at-rest," or shared over a network, and thus be "in-transit." For example, Alice writes and sends an email to Bob. When the email is on its way from Alice's email account to Bob's, the email is data-in-transit, but in the end, one copy of the email is saved in Alice's sent folder and one copy is saved in Bob's inbox, making both copies of the email data-at-rest.

In addition to having two basic states, data also has two basic parts: the content and the metadata. The *content* of the data refers to the substance of the file, the part you read or use, while the *metadata* of the data refers to the information about the data that can be known without opening the file and reading its contents. When you look at a photo stored in your smart phone, you are seeing the content, but you can also access the metadata—information about the photo's size and the date, time, and (increasingly) location of its creation—without looking at the photo itself. Both data-at-rest and data-in-motion have content and metadata. Alice's email to Bob, for instance, has the content of her message ("meet me at the library") and the metadata indicating the size of the email (25 kB), when the email was sent (8:03 AM, 12 July 2018), and the email addresses of both Alice and Bob, the sender and the recipient. Importantly, metadata can be copied and stored separately from its corresponding content. Someone could make a record that Alice sent Bob a 25 kB email at 8:03 AM, 12 July 2018 without having a copy of the message "meet me at the library." If metadata were collected for all their emails, then there would be a database of metadata regarding Alice and Bob's correspondence.

In addition to understanding the states and parts of data, it is also necessary to understand the two basic modes of surveillance: targeted surveillance and mass surveillance. *Targeted surveillance* is the practice of monitoring the activities and communications a specific person or small group. This type of surveillance is often conducted by governmental law enforcement agencies, and in the US, the Fourth Amendment is understood as stipulating standards—such as establishing probable cause and requiring a search warrant—for government agents seeking to conduct this type of surveillance (Rubenfeld 2008). *Mass surveillance*, on the other hand, is the practice of monitoring the activities and communications of entire populations, whether nationally or internationally. Government agencies conduct mass surveillance when they have access to the telecommunication infrastructure and want to indiscriminately collect, store, and analyze data about whole populations. Corporations also conduct mass surveillance, especially large tech firms with millions and billions of users, so they can attempt to predict user interests and present advertisements that users are likely to click on (Zuboff 2019). Increasingly, government agencies and corporations collaborate in their pursuit of mass surveillance practices. Google, Facebook, and other tech giants have a history of providing the NSA and other government agencies access to its databases and cloud storage servers (Greenberg 2012; Greenwald 2014).

Both the targeted and mass modes of surveillance can be used to target the content and the metadata of data in any state. When a government agency conducts targeted surveillance, they can search the contents of a person's computer, collect the contents of a person's emails from their email service, the metadata of a person's phone calls form their cellular carrier, and even install devices that allow them to listen to a person's phone calls in real time. Through this combination of access to content and metadata both at-rest and in-transit, government agents can piece together a thorough image of that person's behaviors, activities, and associates. When governments and corporations conduct mass surveillance, they seek access to all possible data from all relevant persons at all times. Though these mass surveillance organizations often seek access to data content, metadata often provides even more insight into larger patterns of social behavior (de Zwart 2016).

To protect the privacy of data in this modern surveillance context, we can use two types of encryption: symmetric key crypto and asymmetric key crypto. The most used digital crypto with a symmetric key system is Advanced Encryption Standard (AES), developed by Joan Daemen and Vincent Rijmen (1999). The mathematical operations of AES are far more complex than simple substitutions ciphers, but simple substitutions ciphers and AES are both symmetric key ciphers, which means that the same key is used to encrypt and decrypt messages. Because AES is a symmetric key cipher, it is primarily used to encrypt data-at-rest, whether stored on a personal device or in cloud storage. As with all symmetric key ciphers, AES encryption keys must be kept secret. Alice cannot securely send Bob her AES key because Eve could intercept it and use it to decrypt all their messages.

While AES can be used for data-at-rest, asymmetric key crypto or the public key ciphers can be used for data-in-transit (Diffie and Hellman 1976; Rivest et al. 1978). When Alice sends Bob a text message using Short Message Service (SMS), anyone with access to any part of the network can read the plaintext of that message, including their cellular carriers. It is the digital equivalent to sending a postcard: anyone who can see the postcard can read the message written on it. To ensure privacy of their conservation, Alice and Bob can use encrypted messaging apps and other programs to share public encryption keys and thus message securely. It is the digital equivalent to using a sealed envelope to send a letter—except there are no known digital "letter openers" that would allow an eavesdropper to unseal the crypto envelope.

Importantly, public key encryption takes two forms ("Link" 2009). *End-to-end encryption* (E2EE) is used to encrypt the content of data-in-transit while leaving the metadata visible to the network, so it knows where to send the message. E2EE is analogous to a post mail letter in a sealed envelope: the post office cannot read the content of the message because it is sealed inside the envelope, but the post office can read all the metadata—the names and addresses of both sender and recipient, as well as the mark indicating the time, day, and location the letter was mailed. On a network where all users are using E2EE, anyone conducting traffic analysis of all the communication on that network would be able to see the names, addresses, and contacts, so to speak, of everyone communicating on that network, but they would not be able to read any of the messages. *Link encryption*, on the other hand, is used to encrypt the content *and* metadata of data-in-transit along any given "link" of its journey across networks, but this means that the entire message, including the content, must be decrypted at each stop along the way. Otherwise, the servers through which the messages pass would not know where to send the message next. Staying with the post mail analogy, this is the equivalent of putting a letter *and* the addresses inside the envelope knowing that the post office will open the envelope to access the destination address. On a network where all users are using link encryption, all server nodes that forward the messages to recipient devices would be able to decrypt the message and access the content and the metadata, but anyone conducting traffic analysis of all the communication on that network would be *unable* to see the names, addresses, and contacts of everyone communicating on that network. Thus, there is a trade off in terms of privacy. E2EE exposes the metadata of the communication to the network while ensuring that only the intended recipient can access its content, and link encryption conceals the content and metadata of the communication from the network but allows each authorized server node to access both content and metadata. In the end, we can use different types of crypto to secure our data against the various forms of surveillance, but there will be tradeoffs no matter what choices we make.

Anarchy, Justice, Privacy

When it comes to privacy for the weak, one of the major differences between crypto anarchist cypherpunks and crypto justice cypherpunks is the degree of privacy demanded. Crypto anarchists like Tim May (2001b), for example, speak frequently about anonymous and untraceable communications. The second sentence in May's "Crypto Anarchist Manifesto" celebrates the idea that "Computer technology is on the verge of providing the ability for individuals and groups to communicate and interact with each other in a totally anonymous manner" (61). May (2001b) suggests that "privacy" and "anonymity" represent differing degrees of opacity: privacy makes it difficult to be tracked or surveilled, but anonymity makes it impossible. As a crypto anarchist, May concludes that privacy is better than no defense against surveillance, but only complete anonymity will allow individuals to undermine the power of governments. "No longer can nation-states tell their citizen-units what they can have access to," he observes, "not if these citizens can access the cyberspace world through anonymous systems" (75). For May, anonymity means that no person should be compelled to reveal their true name. Though people have a psychological need to "know" who they are interacting with (May 2001c, 71) and governments are motivated by power to know who is doing what with whom (May 2001a, 43), May is clear that only anonymity will lead to crypto anarchy. May's speculations about using crypto to achieve anonymity were always expressed as hopes for the future, not descriptions of present-day fact, and even though several decades have passed since May first articulated the basic ideas of crypto anarchism, complete anonymity is still not possible (May 2018).

Though crypto anarchists desire anonymity, most cypherpunks accept privacy as a sufficient defense against surveillance; however, they argue that we must rethink even our everyday uses of technology, starting with smart phones, social media, and search engines (Assange et al. 2012). All three of these technologies undermine privacy and enable surveillance. "A mobile phone is a tracking device that also makes calls," Assange explains (47). From the user's perspective, a smart phone is designed to complete communication tasks, such as making calls and sending text messages, but from the perspective of manufacturers and service providers, a smart phone is designed to gather data on your location, behaviors, and interests. Social media surveillance is an extension of the smart phone, and apps like Facebook are designed to elicit private information from users; even when the user does not upload photos and make posts, everything they click and swipe is tracked, recorded, and stored forever. As Jérémie Zimmermann notes, Facebook purposefully blurs the lines between privacy and publicity not only for content uploaded by users but also for behavioral data recorded by Facebook (50). While phones and social media enable the extreme surveillance capabilities of large tech companies, Jacob Appelbaum forcefully reminds us that Google—the most used search engine in the world—is "the greatest surveillance machine that ever existed" (69). Google has come to dominate internet search to such a degree that "googling" has become the verb used to refer to the act of searching the internet. There is a danger in giving Google such dominance in both practice and in language, for like Facebook, Google records not only our search queries but also all behavioral data it can access, whether on Google or not. A person who has installed Google and Facebook apps on their smart phone has no privacy because privacy is impossible by design (Zuboff 2019).

Like smart phones, social media, and search engines, cloud storage is an increasingly common daily use technology that threatens privacy (Assange et al. 2012; Van Hoboken 2014). Though cloud storage can be used by individuals and organizations for many different purposes, one of the most ubiquitous uses of the cloud is backing up data from smart phones. From the user's perspective, having a backup of data on the cloud is helpful; if the phone is damaged, lost, or stolen, the owner of the phone still has all their data. In storing their data on a server somewhere, however, the user makes their data vulnerable to third-party surveillance and control. Before Edward Snowden blew the whistle on NSA surveillance in 2013, the NSA had been granted access to the user data stored on the cloud servers of most major tech companies; because the data was not encrypted, the US government was secretly able to read every message, view every picture, and examine all metadata (Greenwald 2014; de Zwart 2016). For their own part, tech companies scanned all user data stored in the cloud to expand their databases of knowledge about user behavioral patterns. Since 2013, most tech companies encrypt their cloud storage, but from the cypherpunk perspective, there is still a problem. If a person backs up their phone data in Google or Apple's encrypted cloud but Google and Apple have access to the AES encryption keys, then the data is *still* not private. Not only could Google and Apple easily decrypt the data without users being aware, they could also share decrypted data with the NSA and other government agencies without users' knowledge. Furthermore, tech companies can claim that a user violated the terms of service and prevent users from accessing their data stored in the cloud; these companies can even delete user data. For these reasons, Andy Müller-Maguhn argues that the cypherpunk role "is to keep [systems] decentralized, have our own infrastructure, not rely on cloud computing and other bullshit, but have our own thing" (76–77). For cypherpunks, data is truly private only if it is stored on a device owned and controlled by the person whose data it is.

While the anti-privacy aspects of social media and cloud storage can be avoided by simply not using them, communication and internet traffic represent an entirely different challenge. Cypherpunks advocate using messaging apps and email services with E2EE, but these services enable only the security of messages-in-transit, not full anonymity. Most of these services require users to authenticate themselves using their real phone numbers, so even though Eve cannot read Alice and Bob's emails and texts when they use these services, Eve could see that Alice and Bob are communicating, how often they communicate, and so on. Likewise, internet traffic is vulnerable to surveillance, and though much of the internet is now encrypted, there are still shortcomings. Most websites are now protected with Hypertext Transfer Protocol Secure (HTTPS), which means that all the traffic between your computer and the website's servers is encrypted; however, your internet service provider (ISP) and other organizations that monitor internet traffic still know you visited that specific website at that time.

The simplest way to obscure your internet traffic is to use a virtual private network (VPN). When using a VPN, your computer or phone establishes an encrypted connection to one server, the VPN server, which then relays all your internet traffic requests. Any Eve monitoring your web traffic will see a single, encrypted connection between your device and one server, and they will not know which websites you are visiting. On the other end, the servers for all the websites you visit will get their traffic requests from the VPN server, not your computer, thereby obscuring your location and identity (if you are not logged into any accounts). Like encrypted email and messaging services, VPNs are not anonymous because users are often required to sign up using their true names. More importantly, even though your ISP and the websites you visit will have more difficulty surveilling you, the VPN provider knows all your traffic. Many VPNs claim to offer total anonymity and promote their services by claiming that they keep no logs of activity, but many such services have been caught lying about their logging practices (Taylor 2017). Still, cypherpunks argue that VPNs offer internet users a greater degree of privacy; as Assange notes, "new networks are being built on top of the internet, virtual private networks, and their privacy comes from cryptography" (Assange et al. 2012, 61).

Even more than VPNs, the cypherpunks advocate the use of the Tor browser (Assange et al. 2012). The Tor Project was originally developed by the US Navy but now exists as a nonprofit organization, though it still receives US government finding (Greenberg 2012). The name Tor comes from the acronym TOR, which is short for "the onion router." The network earned this name because it relies on several layers of encryption with are "peeled back" like layers of an onion. With a VPN, your internet traffic passes through one server node on the way to the destination servers of the websites you visit, but with Tor, your traffic passes through three server nodes on the way to the website servers. Tor traffic is secured under three layers of encryption, and every time the traffic passes through a Tor node, one layer is decrypted and the traffic forwarded to the next node. In other words: after connecting to the Tor network, you type in a web address. That request goes to Tor Node A, where one layer is decrypted. Node A then sees that the traffic is to be send to Node B. When it arrives at Node B, one more layer of encryption is removed, and the traffic is sent to Node C, where the final layer of encryption is removed and the request is sent to the servers of the desired website. Because there are so many nodes, no single node knows everything about the web traffic. Node A knows your device and Node B, but it knows neither Node C nor the destination of the web traffic request. Node B knows Nodes A and C, but it knows neither your device nor the destination of the web traffic. Node C knows Node B and the destination of the web traffic, but it knows neither your device nor Node A. As with a VPN, any eavesdropper monitoring your device's connection will see only a connection to one Tor node. Any eavesdropper watching the fully unencrypted traffic exit Node C will be able to see all traffic, but they will not know the origin of the traffic.

Cypherpunks have used Tor for many projects, including the Silk Road and WikiLeaks, and they advocate the use of Tor by everyone (Assange et al. 2012). But Tor provides no privacy for those who login to personal accounts over the network. For example, there is no point in using Tor and then logging into a personal email account, for by logging in, you reveal your identity. For those who do not login to their accounts, Tor provides what is likely the greatest possible level of privacy online, but it is not completely anonymous in the crypto anarchist sense of the term. Thirty years after May (2001b) first articulated the crypto anarchist vision, crypto-enabled anonymity remains impossible, but this has not prevented crypto anarchists from trying, and it has not prevented other cypherpunks from developing, using, and advocating a broad range of privacy-protecting crypto tools.

Cryptocurrencies as Anarchist Cash

Governments and corporations increasingly surveil our communications, but they also surveil our economic transactions. As David Chaum (1985) observes, "Just as tracing data in communication systems allows all of an individual's records with organizations to be linked because they all use the same address, payment data allow linking of records that involve payments with the same account" (1035). Before the digital age, most transactions were conducted using a cash form of fiat currency, which is currency created, backed, and authorized by a government (US dollars, Euros, Yuan). With cash, we can buy goods at a store or pay a friend or neighbor relatively anonymously because there is no centralized ledger where those transactions are recorded. In the digital age, however, whether we are making a purchase at the grocery store or online, we often pay for goods using a credit or debit card. While these transactions are encrypted, preventing snoopers and criminals from recording our card numbers, they are not private. Actually, they negate the privacy enabled by cash because several parties—the bank where you have an account, the retailer where you made the purchase, the companies that facilitate the money transfer (Visa, MasterCard, PayPal), and often various government agencies—keep detailed records of what was purchased, how much money was spent, and the time, day, and location of the transaction. Recognizing that both communications *and* economic activity were equally vulnerable to mass surveillance, the cypherpunks and other cryptographers pursued various crypto tools that would enable economic privacy for the weak in the digital age. The result is what we now call cryptocurrency, with Bitcoin being perhaps the most influential and well known.

The cypherpunks' road to cryptocurrencies was not linear, for it went through several technological and philosophical iterations beginning with the work of David Chaum (1985). As computers became more ubiquitous and financial systems became digitally networked, Chaum realized that our purchasing habits reveal much about us: our movements and locations, our interests and possessions, and our associations and business dealings. Foreseeing a future where most people paid for goods and services over digital networks, Chaum feared that the record of our purchases would enable increased mass surveillance and thus undermine—or eliminate—privacy. Pioneering methods for private online purchases, Chaum started a company called DigiCash, which allowed customers to withdraw fiat currency from a bank account to an encrypted digital "card." That card could then be used to make purchases online without the retailer knowing the true identity of the purchaser and without the bank, credit card companies, or governments having a record of the transaction. "Chaum's DigiCash was transactionally anonymous," Finn Brunton (2019) explains, "even more than banknotes themselves were: once withdrawn from your (named, identified) account at the bank, the money could not be used to connect a purchase to you" (163). In our current economic system, a person goes to an online retailer, enters their card information, and makes a purchase. In Chaum's DigiCash system, a person would use their crypto card as an anonymizing node between the bank and the retailer, simultaneously circumventing the banks and government who would be interested in recording the transaction.

Though Chaum's technological and philosophical contributions created the foundation for the development of cryptocurrencies, DigiCash was not a cryptocurrency as we know them today, and it did not satisfy the nearly universal cypherpunks demand for completely anonymous, non-state digital money. "Chaum's work on untraceable electronic cash," May (2001a) writes, "sparked the realization that a digital economy could be constructed, with anonymity, intractability, and ancillary anarcho-capitalist features" (35). Yet Chaum's DigiCash was simply "a way to create temporary digital versions of existing money"

(Brunton 2019, 157). Chaum argued that DigiCash offered a way to protect fiat currency from fully digital competition: "If we don't get the national currencies in electronic form properly," Chaum warned, "then the market will route around them and make other currencies" (quoted in Brunton 2019, 59). But cypherpunks *want* other currencies. For crypto anarchists like May (2001a), fully untraceable markets and currencies enable individuals to hide their wealth from the coercive taxation powers of the state. But even non-crypto anarchist cypherpunks like Assange argue that creating and using non-state cryptocurrencies undermines the authority of governments and shifts the power balance away from the powerful and toward the weak. According to Assange, state power is enabled by monopolies over military power, communication infrastructure, and financial infrastructure. "If you take away the state's monopoly over the means of economic transaction," he explains, "then you take away one of the three principal ingredients of the state" (Assange et al. 2012, 90). Taking inspiration from Chaum, the cypherpunks worked to move beyond the limitations of DigiCash to create fully stateless cryptocurrencies.

Today, the most influential and successful cryptocurrency is Bitcoin, which was announced in the paper "Bitcoin: A Peer-to-Peer Electronic Cash System," authored under the pseudonym Satoshi Nakamoto (2008). Though some of the technical aspects of Bitcoin, such as "mining," digital signatures, and hash functions are outside the scope of this discussion (see Brunton 2019; Martin 2020), it is possible to establish a general understanding of how this currency works. Bitcoin allows "any two willing parties to transact directly with each other without the need for a trusted third party" by "using a peer-to-peer distributed timestamp server to generate computational proof of the chronological order of transactions" (Nakamoto 2008, 1). The first difference between Bitcoin and a fiat currency like US dollars is the ledger. For US dollars, we rely on a third party, like a bank, to keep a *centralized* ledger or record of all our transactions. If Alice electronically transfers $10 from her bank account to Bob's bank account, the two banks agree that the $10 has moved and they record this transaction in their ledgers. Other people who use US dollars do not know about Alice and Bob's transaction, but the banks know. For Bitcoin, which is P2P, Alice's coin goes directly to Bob without passing through banks. When Alice transfers $10 to Bob, the transaction is recorded on a *distributed* ledger that every Bitcoin user can read because every Bitcoin user has an identical copy of the ledger. Because there is no centralized system of trust, giving everyone a record of all transactions the only way for everyone to agree on how much Bitcoin each person has, and this is done cryptographically. As Keith Martin (2020) helpfully puts it, in a distributed ledger system like Bitcoin's, "you don't need a bank, because you, and everyone else who has money, *are* the bank" (118).

At first glance, Bitcoin's distributed ledger systems seem less private than traditional centralized ledgers, but that is because Bitcoin inverts the privacy mechanisms of traditional ledger. As the original Bitcoin paper explains:

> The traditional banking model achieves a level of privacy by limiting access to information to the parties involved and the trusted third party. The necessity to announce all transactions publicly precludes this method, but privacy can still be maintained by breaking the flow of information in another place: by keeping public keys anonymous.
>
> (Nakamoto 2008, 6)

Bitcoin uses Whitfield Diffie and Martin Hellman's (1976) public key crypto method, but it changes what others know about the keys. When it comes to encrypting communication, Alice shares her public key and tells everyone that it is hers so they can send her private messages. When it comes to Bitcoin, public keys, which are called Bitcoin addresses, are not publicly associated with the identities of the owners. Thus, if Alice sends Bob one Bitcoin, the distributed ledger will show that one public key sent one Bitcoin to another public key, but Alice and Bob's names appear nowhere in the ledger. All Bitcoin users can see—and, because of the mathematical operations that make the ledger work, *agree*—that one key sent one coin to another key without knowing the true names and identities of Alice and Bob, the key owners. Thus, Bitcoin is built around a system in which the user creates "an anonymous account" but exchanges money that is "unconditionally visible, traceable, and public" (Brunton 2019, 163).

For cypherpunks, Bitcoin is quite exciting and useful, but it fails to satisfy the cypherpunk demand for anonymous transactions. Unlike Chaum's DigiCash, Bitcoin is a non-state currency. When Bitcoin users transact, they do not exchange fiat currency like US dollars; instead, their value exchanged is in the *bits*, the *cryptographic data itself*. Cypherpunks have put Bitcoin to good use. In 2011, for example, when Visa, MasterCard, and PayPal imposed a financial blockade on WikiLeaks, supporters could and did circumvent this blockade by donating Bitcoin (Benkler 2011; Assange et al. 2012). Yet problems remain. One problem is that most people who own Bitcoin use it as an investment option, not as a currency for making everyday purchases

(Grabowski 2019). Another problem is that Bitcoin has increasingly come under the control of national laws, which represent the intention of governments to control or regulate this non-state currency. From a technological perspective, Bitcoin does not require identification, but from a legal perspective, Bitcoin users are required to disclose their identities to get full access to Bitcoin transactions (Grabowski 2019; Prathap 2021). Of course, even without mandatory identification policies, governments can trace Bitcoin transactions back to their participants through pattern analysis: if Alice's identifiable behavior matches a pattern of behavior corresponding to an anonymous Bitcoin public key, the authorities are likely to conclude that the key is Alice's. The cypherpunks recognize this, and they hope that cryptocurrencies continue to evolve into truly anonymous systems (Assange et al. 2012).

For his own part, May (2018) is alarmed by the direction Bitcoin is going. "I can't speak for what Satoshi intended," he says:

> but I sure don't think it involved bitcoin exchanges that have draconian rules...and laws about reporting 'suspicious activity' to the local secret police. There's a real possibility that all the noise about 'governance,' 'regulation' and 'blockchain' will effectively create a surveillance state, a dossier society.

In other words, government efforts to regulate Bitcoin combined with the willingness of Bitcoin managers to cooperate means that Bitcoin might become a surveillance tool, the opposite of what Nakamoto intended. "Sorry if this ruins the narrative," May concludes, "but I think the narrative is fucked. Satoshi did a brilliant thing, but the story is far from over."

Conclusion

Though the crypto anarchist dream of totally anonymous and untraceable communications and transactions remains out of reach, this has not stopped cypherpunks from advocating privacy for the weak. Whether developing and using cryptographic tools like Tor or Bitcoin, cypherpunks remain committed to maximizing the benefits of the digital-information age while minimizing the threat of surveillance. Of course, given the anti-privacy position of governments and corporations, those in power continually seek to frighten publics into surrendering privacy in exchange for some vague feeling of safety or security. Whenever crypto becomes widely used in defense of privacy for the weak, anti-privacy propaganda will proliferate, stories about terrorists, kidnappers, money launderers, drug dealers—or as the cypherpunks refer to them in jest, the Four Horsemen of the Infopocalypse (Assange et al. 2012). Such fear monger tactics are often successful, for as May observes, most people vacillate between proclaiming "None of your business" and "I have nothing to hide" (Levy 2001, 252). Even those who strongly insist on privacy will sometimes capitulate when the Four Horsemen of the Infopocalypse are on the loose.

While crypto anarchists are primarily interested in advancing an individualistic, libertarian conception of freedom from coercive states, crypto justice cypherpunks are more interested in community self-determination on the national and regional scale. Such cypherpunks argue that crypto can be used by weaker states to resist the imperial policies of western powers (Assange 2013; Avila et al. 2017). The distinction between anarchy and justice on this point is crucial, for not only do western powers conduct mass surveillance against the citizens of small, formerly colonized nations in Latin America, Africa, and Asia, but they also use mass surveillance to conduct lethal strikes with weaponized drones. Noting that former NSA Director Michael Hayden admitted that "we kill people based on metadata," Phillip Rogaway (2015) observes that "surveillance and assassination by drones are one technological ecosystem" (113). When we expand the notion of "privacy for the weak" to account for racial and colonial violence, we see that privacy and surveillance are not simply about whose emails are read without person. For the victims of empire, it is a matter of life and death (Gürses et al. 2016; Rexhepi 2016).

Importantly, it is no coincidence that the largest and most powerful surveillance organizations—NSA, Google, Facebook—are also the most secretive. As Adam Moore (2011) reminds us, "One marker of power is the ability to demand information disclosures from others while keeping one's own information secret" (152). Thus, cypherpunks demand privacy for the weak not because they view privacy as some vague right but because it alters the balance of power in favor of individuals, communities, and small organizations. Likewise, many cypherpunks demand transparency for the powerful, going on the offensive to reveal the secrets of those who control the political and economic institutions of the twenty-first century.

6 Transparency for the Powerful

Introduction

Privacy for the weak is a necessary principle for surveillance self-defense in the digital age, but for many cypherpunks, it is only half of the equation. Using crypto to promote privacy can be considered a *re*-active form of data activism because it is primarily defensive, but the cypherpunks also advocate an offensive, *pro*-active form of data activism, and it is captured by the second half of their guiding slogan: *privacy for the weak, transparency for the powerful* (Milan and van der Velden, 2016; Anderson 2021).

In its early years, the cypherpunks often focused on privacy for the weak, but when Julian Assange created WikiLeaks in 2006, he brought transparency for the powerful to the forefront of the movement. Alongside encrypted messaging apps and cryptocurrencies, WikiLeaks stands as one of the most important cypherpunk creations. Assange (2006) argues that the governments and corporations who do the most harm—either through mass surveillance, economic control, or direct military violence—use secrecy to hide their nefarious plans and thereby prevent publics from organizing opposition movements. Because he conceives of governments and corporations as conspiratorial computational networks that carry out their harmful plans by processing external data and communicating internally, Assange concludes that information leaks disrupt the ability of conspiracies to operate effectively. "We have come to the conclusion," Assange wrote at the moment of WikiLeaks' founding, "that fomenting a worldwide movement of mass leaking is the most effective political intervention available to us" (quoted in Greenberg 2012, 131). For Assange (2016), WikiLeaks was designed precisely to promote justice. In one early recruitment email, Assange sought "good people, courageous people" interested in building "an engine for justice" (Greenberg 2012, 97–98).

DOI: 10.4324/9781003220534-6

Thus, the WikiLeaks slogan: "The method is transparency. The goal is justice" (quoted in Hayase 2016). In an age when the all-seeing eyes of a transnational surveillance dystopia pose an existential threat to privacy for the weak, Assange views crypto as the best defense of one's privacy, but he also views crypto as the best offense, using it to impose transparency upon the conspiratorial governments, corporations, and agencies can comprise that dystopia. By making public what was meant to be a secret of the powerful, WikiLeaks provides a means of enforcing transparency for the powerful.

WikiLeaks has been highly effective at imposing transparency upon secretive organizations, and for this reason, Assange has been subjected to a decade-long program of persecution by the US and UK governments. After publishing its first documents in December 2006, WikiLeaks spent the next three years publishing documents from major banks and governments including Kenya, Iceland, US, and many others (Assange 2011). In 2010, however, WikiLeaks began publishing documents, provided by an army private named Chelsea Manning, that exposed US government lies and war crimes in Iraq and Afghanistan. These publications were followed by the release of US State Department cables, also provided by Manning. In response, the US government sought to capture Assange and shutdown WikiLeaks using any means necessary. In early 2011, Assange began what would become a decade of incarceration—more than a year under house arrest, followed by almost seven years trapped in the Ecuadorian embassy in London, followed by approximately three years in Belmarsh prison, where he remains at the time of this publication—all without having been convicted of a crime. During this decade of incarceration, the US government partnered with wealthy individuals and private security firms to install cameras and microphones in the Ecuadorian embassy, recording his every action and his conversations with doctors, lawyers, and family members (Blumenthal 2020). The US government also considered kidnapping or even assassinating Assange (Dorfman et al. 2021). This coordinated program of persecution, incarceration, harassment, and surveillance not only violated Assange's human rights but also subjected him to what the United Nations Special Rapporteur on Torture called "psychological torture" (Addley 2014; "UN expert" 2019; Melzer 2019).

The sections that follow situate WikiLeaks within the cypherpunk movement and explore two philosophical ways that Assange has explained his whistleblowing and publishing platform. The first section provides a short intellectual genealogy of cypherpunk "information markets." Assange was not the first cypherpunk to imagine ways of using crypto to impose transparency on the powerful. In fact, we can trace this idea from Tim May's BlackNet, through the thought of Jim Bell, John Young, Ross Ulbricht, and ultimately Assange. From this perspective, we can appreciate why, when WikiLeaks began publishing the documents leaked by Manning, science fiction writer Bruce Sterling (2010) proclaimed, "At last—at long last—the homemade nitroglycerin in the old cypherpunks blast shack has gone off." The second section explains WikiLeaks cybernetic function, namely, introducing untraceable leaks into the environment of conspiratorial communication networks. Using crypto, WikiLeaks not only protects whistleblowers from backlash but also causes conspiracies to contract. The third section explores WikiLeaks' journalistic philosophy, what Assange calls "scientific journalism." According to Assange, journalists ought to report based on authentic documents, and they ought to make those documents available to the public so readers can decide for themselves if the journalist's report is accurate. By situating WikiLeaks properly, we can better understand how Assange's creation reflects cypherpunks ethics and why it has been so effective at promoting transparency for the powerful.

Information, Markets, and Information Markets

"BlackNet is in the business of buying, selling, trading, and otherwise dealing with *information* in all its forms," Tim May (1996a) writes of his concept for a crypto-enabled information black market. May's hypothetical information market would build an "information inventory" of trade secrets, product plans, business intelligence, and documents concerning the design and production of everything from semiconductors to pharmaceuticals to "children's toys" and "cruise missiles." Using various layers of crypto, BlackNet would provide users with "a secure, two-way, untraceable, and fully anonymous channel" for the sale of stolen or otherwise obtained secret information from government, corporations, and any other parties unwise enough to leave their data unencrypted. BlackNet users would be paid in a special cryptocurrency called "CryptoCredits," which could be used to purchase black market information from other anonymous sellers or perhaps cashed out to spend elsewhere online (241–242). In May's (1996b) view, the existence of strong digital public key crypto would lead necessarily to a world in which it would be increasingly difficult for large organizations to either keep secrets or track down those responsible for leaking and selling them. As he put it in no uncertain terms:

crypto-anarchy doesn't mean a "no secrets" society; it means a society in which individuals must protect their own secrets and not count on governments or corporations to do it for them. It also means "public secrets," like troop movements and Stealth production plans, or the tricks of implanting wafers, will not remain secret for long.

(247–248)

May's BlackNet was inspired by Phillip Salin's idea for the American Information Exchange (AMIX), an early version of an online marketplace for intellectual property (Brunton 2019). In Salin's vision, AMIX would provide an online marketplace where businesses and individuals could auction information of any kind to willing bidders and buyers. Salin believed that more individuals and organizations would share information if they could be financially compensated for such information. Those involved with AMIX, Salin said, were "just trying to reduce the friction and transaction costs that keep people from trading their knowledge for gain" (quoted in Brunton 2019, 70). While Salin believed that financial incentives could incentivize businesses into sharing information, May (1996b) argued that corporations would not tolerate such information markets. Not only do businesses retain their competitive advantage by keeping "trade secrets" secret, May insisted, they also prohibit employees from acting on behalf of the company without proper authorization, and no company would authorize employees to sell business secrets. In conceiving of AMIX, Salin had also overlooked the power of crypto, and for May, the potential for crypto to create anonymous exchanges meant that information black markets would become almost inevitable. Hundreds of employees at Northrop Grumman have access to the design plans of the B-2 Spirit Stealth Bomber, May notes, but they do not leak or sell such information because they are watched closely by management and government agents. But with crypto, the same employees could potentially sell B-2 plans without being caught.

While May's BlackNet essays introduced the notion of "information markets" to the movement, other cypherpunks would take this idea in different directions. Some cypherpunks emphasized the *market* half of "information markets" and created some of the most controversial ideas—both hypothetical and implemented—to emerge from the movement. Shortly after May's BlackNet essays appeared, Jim Bell spent a year penning "Assassination Politics," which envisioned an online marketplace where users could anonymously bet on which day a government official would be assassinated. May (1996b) briefly noted that BlackNet-type platforms could lead to "liquid markets for killing and extortion" (248), and Bell sought to provide a full conceptualization of this possibility. As Bell (1997) explained, government officials guilty of violating the rights of the people would be the primary targets for the platform: "the 'victim' is a government employee, presumably one who is not merely taking a paycheck of stolen tax dollars, but also is guilty of extra violations of rights beyond this," mentioning the Ruby Ridge and Waco incidents as examples. Whenever a rights-violating government official was assassinated, the assassination marketplace would pay the anonymous person who correctly "predicted" the day of the assassination, implying that the assassin him or herself were the ones to collect the cryptocurrency bounty. Bell expended much effort to untangling the ethical, legal, technical, and logistical issues with his hypothetical assassination market, which he hoped would enable publics to hold politicians accountable. Neither Bell nor anyone else ever built it (Greenberg 2012).

Bell was not the only cypherpunk to pursue the *market* in "information markets." In 2011, Ross Ulbricht—using the handle Dred Pirate Roberts—launched the Silk Road, a dark web marketplace where users could anonymously buy and sell illegal objects and controlled substances. Silk Road could only be accessed through the Tor network, and all transactions were made using Bitcoin. Ulbricht wrote that he wanted "to create a website where people could buy anything anonymously, with no trail whatsoever that could lead back to them" (quoted in Bearman 2015a). Under Ulbricht's direction, Silk Road became "a multimillion-dollar drug operation" in under two years (Bearman 2015a). Though Ulbricht specifically cites May's BlackNet as an inspiration for the Silk Road (Brunton 2019), the market's terms of service banned the sale of anything designed "to harm or defraud, such as stolen credit cards, assassinations, and weapons of mass destruction" (Chen 2011). Like May, Ulbricht's public comments suggest that he opposes not unjust governments but governments as such. In his view, activists who seek to decriminalize drugs simply give the state power to tax drug transactions. Thus, Silk Road provided an alternative to both the war on drugs and the legalization of drugs by creating a crypto-enabled drug market outside the purview of the state. Or so it seemed. Despite rhetoric to the contrary, Tor and Bitcoin are not completely anonymous, and in late 2013, the Silk Road was shut down by the US government (Chen 2011; Greenberg 2013; Bearman 2015a, 2015b).

While Bell and Ulbricht took up the "market" aspect of May's BlackNet, other cypherpunks took up the "information" aspect. The first cypherpunk information *platform*, rather than market, was Cryptome.org, created by John Young and Deborah Natsios in 1996. Cryptome's mission statement has stated that it "welcomes documents for publication that are prohibited by governments worldwide, in particular, material on freedom of expression, privacy, cryptology, dual-use technologies, national security, intelligence and secret governance—but not limited to those" (Golianopoulos 2010). Guided by a "radical anti-secrecy ethos," Young and Natsios have described their platform as "a free public library, rather than a product for sale," thus distinguishing their publishing practices from the market-oriented conceptions of May, Bell, and Ulbricht (Rosen 2014). Despite publishing thousands of very controversial documents—including detailed maps of a US Vice President's secret bunker—Young and Natsios have not articulated a philosophical orientation for Cryptome. They warn potential sources not to reveal themselves, for Cryptome has no means of protecting whistleblowers; they warn potential readers not to trust what they find published on the website, for Cryptome does not provide "context" for the documents it hosts (Greenberg 2012; Crary 2013). In a sense, Cryptome is governed by one motto: "Do not trust the Internet. Do not trust professionals. Do not trust us, or anybody else" (Grima 2011). Though Young and Natsios sort through the documents they received and toss out anything that looks forged, when it comes to what is "true," they tell everyone who visits the site: "It's up to you to decide" (Crary 2013).

When Julian Assange founded WikiLeaks, he followed Young and Natsios in rejecting a market-based model for information, choosing instead an information platform model. Assange sought to join the fight for transparency as early as the 1990s, though it would take him a number of years to develop the full philosophical basis for WikiLeaks. To promote justice in an increasingly unjust world, Assange (2006) sought to use whistleblowing as a means of undermining the power of governments and corporations to harm publics. Cryptome exerted great influence over the philosophy of WikiLeaks. Not only did WikiLeaks' website originally refer to John Young as "the godfather of online leaking," Young agreed to register the wikileaks.org domain in his name (Greenberg 2012). Though Assange's ideas emerge from the genealogy of cypherpunk theories of information and markets, WikiLeaks represents an important shift in cypherpunk ethics. May, Bell, Ulbricht, and other libertarian cypherpunks prioritize individual freedom, market-based relationships, and the minimization or elimination of government, thereby viewing transparency as incidental, ineffective, or irrelevant. Assange, however, concludes that transparency is the most effective means for reconfiguring information flows and achieving a state of justice. Likewise, Assange's conception of transparency moves beyond the insurgent but *ad hoc* approach embodied by Cryptome. By combining insights from cybernetics, political theory, journalism ethics, and other fields, Assange (2006, 2011) developed an elaborate but compelling understanding of how cypherpunks can achieve transparency for the powerful.

WikiLeaks I: Leaks and Conspiracies

WikiLeaks is a whistleblowing platform where government and corporate insiders can go to leak confidential, secret, or otherwise heavily controlled or suppressed documents. Using crypto, the website is designed so whistleblowers can upload documents anonymously so they can be posted online, accessible to anyone who wants to read them. In the original design of WikiLeaks, traffic between the website and the user's computer was encrypted, just like any banking website or online retailer, and the website kept no logs of visitor IP addresses. To further obscure traffic and hide whistleblower identities, the website also included a script that ran artificial upload commands, making it look like every visitor was uploading documents. As Andy Greenberg (2012) succinctly explains, "To anyone snooping on WikiLeaks' visitors, it would be impossible to distinguish between those who had come to the site to read its publications or make a donation and those who intended to drop secrets. Thanks to the cover traffic of spoofed submissions, everyone looked like a leaker" (157). By designing WikiLeaks with an encrypted submission system, Assange (2016) sought to make the whistleblowing process as anonymous as is possible on the internet, thereby reducing the risk to whistleblowers and thus lowering the "courage threshold" (143).

WikiLeaks is constructed as a living embodiment of "privacy for the weak, transparency for the powerful." Just as cypherpunks argues that any individual ought to defend their privacy using crypto, WikiLeaks uses crypto and other methods to protect the privacy of whistleblowers who provide documentary evidence of government and corporate wrongdoing. "Deniability is not just a word," Assange (2011) insists, "it's a way of life and a programme" (163). As the treatment of high-profile whistleblowers like Edward Snowden and Chelsea Manning demonstrates, whistleblowers are among "the weak" in cypherpunk terminology. The cases of John Kiriakou and Gina Haspel are illustrative. Both Kiriakou and Haspel worked for the Central Intelligence Agency (CIA) during the time it practiced what was euphemistically called "enhanced interrogation techniques"—torture, particularly waterboarding. Kiriakou refused to authorize or participate in CIA torture practices, and after leaving the agency, he blew the whistle. After several years of harassment, intimidation, and investigation by the US government, Kiriakou was sentenced to 30 months in prison for revealing classified material (Schmidt 2013). Haspel, on the other hand, oversaw and participated in the torture program at a CIA black site and later destroyed the videotape evidence in violation of court orders. She was later promoted to CIA director by President Donald Trump (Greenwald 2017). In this unjust scenario, the torturer was rewarded and the whistleblower was punished. By protecting whistleblowers, Assange hopes to advance the cause of justice.

While WikiLeaks uses crypto to protect whistleblowers and promote privacy for the weak, it also uses crypto to impose transparency upon the powerful. Remember that Assange's (2006) cybernetic theory of the state and of corporations conceives of these institutions as communication networks consisting of *nodes* (the people in the network) and *links* (all the lines of communication between all the people in the network). For Assange, these communication networks are conspiratorial because they use secrecy to conceal their activities from those outside the network, which in most cases are all the publics that are harmed by conspiracies. Because these conspiratorial networks are thinking things, in a sense, Assange argues that there are three methods of making harder for a conspiracy to think. We can *blind* or *deceive* a conspiracy by denying it accurate information about its environment, making it unable to respond to charging contexts. This measure is essentially achieved through privacy for the weak, for whenever a person encrypts their communications or a whistleblower uses an encrypted submission system, the conspiracy is denied information about its environment.

Likewise, we can *separate* the conspiracy either by eliminating the most important nodes or by cutting the heaviest communication links. This strategy, however, comes with challenges. On the one hand, most modern governments and corporations place individuals "in office," and while it may be possible to eliminate a node by driving someone from their given station, their position is often immediately filled by the next functionary of the conspiracy, thus maintaining the node. Modern conspiracies are also somewhat decentralized, which means that conspiracies are designed to survive the elimination of individual nodes (Bady 2010). Interestingly, in what is almost a direct reference to Jim Bell, Assange (2006) rules out assassination as an acceptable method, suggesting that it is a primitive practice unworthy of enlightened human beings. On the other hand, cutting important links is perhaps easier, but one must have an accurate map of the conspiracy network to know which links to target. Such mapping depends upon the opacity of the conspiracy and the availability of prior information, and no conspiracy willingly supplies its adversaries with a map of itself. Yet without an accurate map, targeting links remains a guessing game.

Though Assange (2006) does not rule out separation, he seems to emphasize a third method: *throttling* or slowing down the speed, efficiency, and clarity with which the conspiracy communicates with itself internally. Modern conspiracies are enormous bureaucracies; they depend on written communication to work effectively, which means that all modern conspiracies leave a paper trail. If any insider leaks a portion of that paper trail, the conspiracy's internal communication become exposed, and the conspiracy has to implement measures to better control and monitor its members. Some critics of WikiLeaks have wrongly concluded that, because Assange is a "hacker" (that word doesn't mean what they think it means), WikiLeaks personnel steal the documents themselves. This interpretation fails to account for Assange theory of throttling a conspiracy. If a conspiracy loses documents to an outside threat, then it will simply reinforce its external defenses, but if a conspiracy loses documents because an insider to the conspiracy *leaks* documents to the outside, then the conspiracy must turn inward, against itself, to find and fix the leak. If a document is leaked and only five members of the conspiracy had access to that document, then the conspiracy would be able to quickly narrow down the culprit, but in a conspiracy like the US government, in which over 5 million people have security clearances, tens of thousands people might have access to the leaked document, thereby making the whistleblower increasingly difficult to identify (Assange 2015). By facilitating leaks, then, WikiLeaks introduces a distinctive threat to the environment of any conspiracy.

It is important to emphasize the leaks in themselves, for even though the *content* of the documents has a role in Assange's vision for WikiLeaks, the *formal* existence of simple, anonymous channels for leaking documents imposes a cost on secret networks that intend to carry out harmful actions. Setting aside for a moment *what* is revealed by leaked documents, one of the novel purposes of WikiLeaks is that the very disclosure of secret documents causes the conspiracy to contract. As Aaron Bady (2010) explains:

> the idea is that increasing the porousness of the conspiracy's information system will impede its functioning, that the conspiracy will turn against itself in self-defense, clamping down on its own information flows in ways that will then impede its own cognitive function. You destroy the conspiracy, in other words, by making it so paranoid of itself that it can no longer conspire…[WikiLeaks] is trying to strangle the links that make the conspiracy possible, to expose the necessary porousness of the American state's conspiratorial network in hopes that the security state will then try to shrink its computational network in response, thereby making itself dumber and slower and smaller.

Interestingly, WikiLeaks' publications of leaked documents have successfully throttled conspiracies, especially the operations of the US government. The hundreds of thousands of documents leaked by Manning, for example, had precisely this effect, for the US government went to great lengths to prevent future leaks of that type and magnitude (Anderson 2020). As the *New York Times* reported in 2010:

> The Defense Department is scaling back information sharing, which its leaders believe went too far after information hoarding was blamed for the failure to detect the Sept. 11 plot. The department has also stripped CD and DVD recorders from its computers; it is redesigning security systems to require two people, not one, to move large amounts of information from a classified computer to an unclassified one; and it is installing software to detect downloads of unusual size.
>
> (Shane 2010)

What's more, the Pentagon created an automatic email filter to block all incoming and outgoing emails containing the word "WikiLeaks," which prevented Pentagon prosecutors from receiving important information related to Manning's prosecution (Assange 2015). Bank of America reacted similarly when it was rumored that WikiLeaks planned to publish leaked documents from the financial giant (Greenberg 2012). Thus, WikiLeaks has successfully used the existence of leaks and the threat of future leaks to throttle several conspiracies.

Building upon his cybernetic theory of the state and other organizations, Assange concludes that it is possible to use crypto in the service of imposing transparency upon the powerful. Conceiving of governments and corporations as connected graphs of communication networks, Assange argues that it is possible to undermine secret conspiratorial networks by making virtually untraceable leaks part of their environment. WikiLeaks is designed to fulfill this function, using an encrypted submission system to protect whistleblowers from being identified and punished by the conspiracy. Though Assange originally prioritized blinding and throttling as the most effective methods of challenging conspiracies, as WikiLeaks publishes more and more documents, it becomes increasingly possible to understand the topography of conspiratorial networks and thus map their links and nodes. *The WikiLeaks Files* was one such exercise, and scholars of surveillance studies have offered similar mappings (van der Vlist 2017; Burke 2020). By making information leaks an environmental threat to conspiracies, Assange hopes that WikiLeaks will thwart the harmful, unjust plans of conspiracies.

WikiLeaks II: Scientific Journalism

In early 2010, when WikiLeaks was busy publishing the documents provided by Chelsea Manning, Assange began using the term "scientific journalism" to describe WikiLeaks' specific publishing method. During WikiLeaks's earliest years, Assange published complete, un-redacted documents online expecting that members of the global reading public would analyze the documents and present their findings (Lynch 2012). When WikiLeaks' publications received less attention than Assange hoped, he began partnering with media outlets around the world to increase the impact of the documents (Assange 2011; Lynch 2013). In these partnerships, Assange was more than a source, for he introduced new standards that were more transparent and rigorous than existing journalistic practices. Assange (2010) explains:

> We work with other media outlets to bring people the news, but also to prove it is true. Scientific journalism allows you to read a news story, then to click online to see the original document it is based on. That way you can judge for yourself: Is the story true? Did the journalist report it accurately?

The evolution of WikiLeaks from a conspiracy-busting facilitator of leaks to a platform for scientific journalism illustrates the growth of the organization and the maturation of Assange's cypherpunk ethics (Brunton 2011). Scientific journalism allows WikiLeaks to continue enforcing transparency for powerful governments and corporations, but it also enables them to impose transparency upon the news media, which all too often gets subsumed into conspiratorial communication networks.

From the perspective of crypto justice, there are two primary problems with traditional news media, or "journalisn't" as Assange (2017) calls it. On the one hand, news media outlets are highly nationalistic rather than cosmopolitan. As Robert Handley and Lou Rutigliano (2012) have found, traditional news publishers, such as the *New York Times*, feel threatened by the kind of new media journalism represented by WikiLeaks. To defend their position within the journalistic field, traditional news publishers reaffirm their relationships to government insiders and increasingly adopt the "national narrative" provided by political elites. Thus, Handley and Rutigliano observe "a tightening of journalistic-state relationships among traditional journalistic outlets as these organizations mark themselves off as 'responsible' national community members vis-à-vis emergent journalistic forms" (746). On the other hand, traditional news publishers almost never publish the documents that inform their reporting, requiring readers to trust that the journalists and editors have reported on events accurately. As Lisa Lynch (2012) describes, most news media journalists rely on an "assertion of journalistic authority in lieu of the inclusion of source material" and thereby expect their audiences to defer to their authority on the reporting at hand (46). Of course, when nationalist commitments and pretenses to journalistic authority are combined, traditional news publishers can cause extreme harm and suffering. The *New York Times*, for instance, published extensively the George W. Bush administration's false claims that Iraq had weapons of mass destruction, leading to a war in which over a million Iraqis were killed (Mitchell 2008). Had the *Times* been more adversarial in relation to the government and had audiences been able to read the documents purporting to substantiate claims that Iraq had such weapons, the war may have been prevented.

As an organization informed by cypherpunk ideals, WikiLeaks stands in contrast to the nationalist tendencies and presumptions of authority expressed by traditional news publishers. As Geoffroy de Lagasnerie (2019) has observed, WikiLeaks embodies "a practical critique of all forms of nationalism," for it is "a project that transcends the idea of nations, and it works to dissolve the nationalistic basis at the root of all conservatisms." WikiLeaks has this character, de

Lagasnerie adds, because Assange is "one of those rare contemporary political figures to adopt truly global perception of the world" (294). Assange's (2011) own words support de Lagasnerie's commentary. Assange eschews the slogan "Think Globally, Act Locally," favoring instead the alternative: Think Globally, Act Globally (Anderson 2020). Assange thus calls WikiLeaks "a post-state organization" and "a stateless media organization" (Assange et al. 2012, 126). Assange also refuses to confine those who might benefit from or contribute to WikiLeaks' journalistic enterprise to any particular nation-state. Instead, when he conceived of WikiLeaks, Assange (2011) believed that "the flow of information would not be a matter for single journalists alone, or for individual media organisations, but for societies working together" (114).

Likewise, Assange rejects the notion that journalists have any special epistemic or professional prerogative to unilaterally decide on behalf of publics which stories are newsworthy and how such stories ought to be reported. Assange therefore calls his style of publishing "scientific journalism" because it is modeled on academic science, in which scholars make their data available to colleagues who can then check verify the work. "If you publish a paper on DNA," he notes, "you are required, by all the good biological journals, to submit the data that has informed your research—the idea being that people will replicate it, check it, verify it. So this is something that needs to be done for journalism as well" (Khatchadourian 2010). Essentially, he is calling for journalism to be subjected to the same evidentiary standards as academia: "things must be precisely cited with the original source, and as much of the information as possible should be put in the public domain so that people can look at it, just like in science so that you can test to see whether the conclusion follows from the experimental data" (Assange 2016, 130). As John C. O'Day (2019) incisively notes, scientific journalism

> considerably ups the ante in terms of professional accountability for journalists. While corporate media are content with sourcing 'people familiar with the documents,' for WikiLeaks obtaining and publishing those documents is not just a bonus or a lucky break, it is a requirement.

In the print age of news media, paper costs and mere matters of space made it nearly impossible for journalists to include the primary sources with every report, but in the digital age, with its exponentially expanding capacities for data storage, there is now no technological or logistical impediment to the practice of scientific journalism.

By avoiding nationalist entanglements and by using scientific journalism to empower readers to check the work of journalists, WikiLeaks shifts the power balance away from governments and corporations to various publics globally. The strongest evidence for this is the influence of Manning and Assange on the 2003 Iraq War. In 2008, Barack Obama campaigned on a policy of withdrawal from Iraq, but as late at 2011, he was looking to negotiate an extended US occupation of Iraq. The documents published by WikiLeaks made such negotiation impossible, forcing Obama to withdraw troops (Greenwald 2011; Avila et al. 2017). For Assange, this event represents an important truth. "Most wars in the twentieth century started as a result of lies amplified and spread by the mainstream press," Assange (2016) observes. While most observers focus on the travesties wrought by such propaganda, Assange sees a silver lining. If publics have to be lied into wars, he argues, then that means "that populations basically don't like wars and they have to be lied into it. That means we can be 'truthed' into peace. That is cause for great hope" (130–131). In this high-profile case, WikiLeaks imposed transparency on the powerful and enabled the publics who would oppose the conspiracy to fight back and thwart the conspiracy's plans for continued occupation—at least in that moment.

Assange prides himself on practicing scientific journalism at WikiLeaks, but in the end, he argues that this method of publishing ought to become the standard practice in all journalism "The press has never been very good," Assange (2016) demurs, but "the condition of the mainstream press nowadays is so appalling, I don't think it can be reformed. I don't think that is possible. I think it has to be eliminated, and replaced with something that's better" (130). Leaks therefore are not only useful for throttling conspiracies but they also provide the textual, documentary basis for the transformation of the political and epistemic basis of journalism itself. And WikiLeaks continues to evolve, for its massive document archives provide researchers with valuable primary sources, just as research libraries do. As WikiLeaks' Sarah Harrison (2015) explains, "An understanding of our historical record enables self-determination; publishing and ensuring easy access to full archives, rather than just individual documents, is central to preserving this historical record" (146). By maintaining document archives and keeping them accessible to people all over the world, WikiLeaks also functions as a library, freeing the world's information.

Conclusion

Though varied in their reasons and their aims, the cypherpunks are somewhat united regarding their commitment to *privacy for the weak*.

When it comes to *transparency for the powerful*, however, there is wide disagreement. May's BlackNet introduced the notion of using crypto to create information black markets, and other cypherpunks took this notion in many directions. Bell and Ulbricht emphasized the "market" idea, developing—and in Ulbricht's case, implementing—these markets in assassination lotteries and illicit drug trade. Ulbricht was more interested in protecting a kind of market privacy for the weak, while Bell was interested not in transparency but violence and death for the powerful. With Cryptome and WikiLeaks, Young and Assange took a different route, creating platforms for suppressed information that promoted transparency. While Assange took inspiration from Cryptome, WikiLeaks is not merely derivative. Assange coupled his mathematical skills with his interest in networks and his desire to see a more transparent world to create an encrypted leaking tool designed to blind and throttle state and corporate conspiracies. After a time, Assange made explicit the implicit journalistic function of WikiLeaks, developing an ethics of scientific journalism that empowers readers and raises the standards of journalistic integrity. WikiLeaks has seen success in both its cybernetic function and its journalistic function, and Assange's ongoing persecution is evidence of this success.

While WikiLeaks has excelled among its cypherpunk platform siblings, this has not resulted in Assange receiving admiration from all other cypherpunks. Young accused Assange of being seduced by fame and wealth (Golianopoulos 2010); he also accused WikiLeaks of being in cahoots with the CIA (Assange 2011). Young ended his short tenure on WikiLeaks' advisory board after Assange notified him of a plan to raise money; in his email, Young wrote, "Fuck your cute hustle and disinformation campaign against legitimate dissent. Same old shit, working for the enemy" (Greenberg 2012, 132). While Young was willing to be part of WikiLeaks for at least a few months, May has expressed his distaste for the politics of WikiLeaks. When asked why May never used his cypherpunk ethics and technical skills in crypto to build a whistleblowing and publishing platform, May explained, "I'm not concerned about things like that. Let the Africans kill each other. I don't have those kinds of political interests...the idea of trying to be Julian Assange gives me the creeps" (Greenberg 2012, 91). May's comment captures a fundamental difference between crypto anarchy and crypto justice. Assange uses crypto to push the entire world toward a state of justice, which entails curtailing western imperialism and undermining authoritarianism wherever it maybe, while May is primarily interested in using crypto as arenas of realizing a kind of elite, individualistic—white and western—autonomy.

These criticisms of WikiLeaks notwithstanding, many contemporary cypherpunks have been highly supportive of WikiLeaks and instrumental in its operations. Jacob Appelbaum, who for a long time was a leader on the Tor project, helped WikiLeaks during the publication of the Manning documents. For Appelbaum, the decision to support or oppose WikiLeaks reveals where one stands on the future. As he asks: "if I don't support Julian now, in the things that he is going through, what kind of world am I building? What kind of message do I send when I let a bunch of pigs push me around?" (Assange et al. 2012, 151–152). Assange has also received praise outside cypherpunk circles. Glenn Greenwald (2021) writes:

> Julian Assange is a pioneer of modern journalism, a visionary who was the first to see that a major vulnerability of corrupt power centers in the digital age was mass data leaks that could expose their misconduct. Based on that prescient recognition, he created a technological and journalistic system to enable noble sources to safely blow the whistle on corrupt institutions by protecting their anonymity: a system now copied and implemented by major news organizations around the world.
>
> (see also Di Salvo 2020)

Though Assange remains a political prisoner, his ideas have truly changed the world. "There are few original ideas in politics," says Robert Manne (2011). "In the creation of WikiLeaks, Julian Assange was responsible for one."

7 Information Wants to Be Free

Introduction

Now that we have understood crypto through a cypherpunk philosophy of technology, explored the philosophies of crypto anarchy and crypto justice, and examined the various ways that cypherpunks have put "privacy for the weak, transparency for the powerful" into practice, we can return to the idea that *all information should be free*. In the introduction, I established a distinction between hackers and cypherpunks, arguing that these two groups, while historically and politically related, offer two very different understandings of information freedom. Whether we consider the academic hackers of the 1960s, the computer hobbyists of the 1970s, or the underground hackers of the 1980s, hackers generally did not make a distinction between "public" and "private" information. This distinction remained, at best, implicit until the cypherpunks made it explicit. For the academic hackers and hobbyists, "information" largely meant software and other technical knowledge (Levy 2010). For the hacker underground, "information" was expanded to include anything that could be known or accessed using computers and networks, including government and corporate files (Sterling 1992). Given these understandings of information, we might say that hackers believed that *all (public) information should be free*. The cypherpunks, however, modified this hacker axiom, bringing out the implicit qualifier "public" and demanding protection for "private" information. This cypherpunk distinction between public and private information is widely accepted by contemporary hacker communities (Chaos Computer Club n.d.), which is why we must note that when hackers today say "all information should be free," what they are really saying is *all public information should be free*.

Just as contemporary hackers accept the cypherpunk position on information freedom, most contemporary cypherpunks consider

DOI: 10.4324/9781003220534-7

themselves hackers. The problem with "hacker" is that popular uses often define the term as someone who commits crimes using computers, but this pejorative meaning of the term was created by corporations, government agents, and traditional news media in order to conflate hackers with computer criminals. Yet even in the golden age of the international hacker underground, hackers who emphasized knowledge and technical skill rarely mixed with "hackers" who committed financial crimes. "There were some hackers who could really steal. And there were hackers who could really hack. But the two groups didn't seem to overlap much, if at all," Bruce Sterling (1992) notes. "Truly heavy-duty hackers, those with serious technical skills who had earned the respect of the underground, never stole money or abused credit cards" (95). Though hackers did find their way into government and corporate computer networks, the best hackers never stole, altered, or destroyed anything (Dreyfus and Assange 2012, 79). When understanding cypherpunks as hackers, then, we must abandon the hacker-as-criminal conception in favor of a better definition. Following Jérémie Zimmermann, we can say, "A hacker is a technology enthusiast, somebody who likes to understand how technology works, not to be trapped into technology but to make it work better" (Assange et al. 2012, 65). And of course, just as all the academic hackers, computer hobbyists, and underground hackers knew, the only way to make technology—and the world more generally—work better is to make information as free and accessible as possible.

Previous chapters examined some cypherpunk methods for defending the private information of the weak, and this chapter will examine the cypherpunks' argument that all public information should be free. For the cypherpunks, censorship is among the most reactionary political and economic practices of the digital age. In the present discussion, *censorship* is defined as any policy, regulation, or enforcement mechanism designed to restrict or prevent individuals' ability to access, read, modify, revise, share, circulate, or otherwise know and communicate public information. In other words, anytime someone prevents you from knowing something or saying something, they are engaged in censorship.

Though some readers might be skeptical of this apparent free speech absolutism, the first section below explores some of the cypherpunks' most compelling arguments against censorship and for information freedom. Most cypherpunks argue that government and corporate secrecy is a form of censorship, and they work to undermine such secrecy using organizations like WikiLeaks to enforce transparency for the powerful. But as the second section explains, cypherpunks also view the enforcement of so-called "intellectual property" restrictions as a particular insidious form of censorship. Such restrictions impede reading, knowing, and communicating and thus for cypherpunks qualify as censorship. The third section below explores two areas where traditional hacker culture and cypherpunk activism blend: the free software and open access movements. While the free software movement seeks to liberate code from the confines of proprietary restrictions so users can read, modify, and share such code, the open access movement seeks to free the world's scientific and academic knowledge from the confines of database paywalls so people everywhere can read and apply humanity's collective knowledge. Returning to our cypherpunk philosophy of technology, not only is crypto convivial but digital information and communication technologies more broadly are convivial to the extent that they promote the freedom of all public information.

On Censorship

To understand the cypherpunk opposition to censorship, let's imagine the benefits of a world without censorship. For the cypherpunks, the first-order benefits are cultural innovation and personal enrichment. No individual creates every idea they think, and even the ideas they do create are built using intellectual material from the existing culture. As Andy Müller-Maguhn observes, "the history of the human race and the history of culture is the history of copying thoughts, modifying and processing them further on" (Assange et al. 2012, 78). By giving the greatest number of people the greatest possible access to information, we promote the greatest number of innovations. Censorship cuts people off from information and therefore limits innovation, but when more people have more access to more information, they can use that information to create new insights, gather new data, and invent new tools—all of which should then be placed into free circulation with the information and knowledge that preceded them. Putting a digital twist on it, Jérémie Zimmermann echoes this notion: "by sharing files between individuals...you build better culture...Culture is meant to be shared" (Assange et al. 2012, 78). But for Zimmermann, sharing does not only improve culture; it improves individuals. "Of course, people say bullshit on the internet—that's obvious," he acknowledges, "but to be able to use this ability to express yourself in public makes you more and more constructed in your way of speaking over time, more and more able to participate in complex discussions" (Assange et al. 2012, 83). In other words, by providing people with a censorship-free space in which to explore their ideas and engaged in dialogue with other about important matters for humanity, they can learn to be thoughtful democratic citizens.

If cultural innovation and personal enrichment are first-order benefits of a censorship-free world, then those benefits contribute to the higher-order end of advancing humanity as much as possible. As Assange (2016) argues, "human civilization, its good part, is based upon our full intellectual record, and our intellectual record should be as large as possible if humanity is to be as advanced as possible" (139). If Assange is correct and human civilization can only be as advanced as humanity's self-knowledge, then the more we make information available to all humans, the more each person can contribute to human advancement. Here, we see the cypherpunk concern about power and communication come full circle, for by freeing information from censorship, we can also redistribute power. "If all the collected information about the world was public," Assange optimistically states, "that might rebalance the power dynamic and let us, as a global civilization, shape our destiny" (Assange et al. 2012, 158). In our current global situation, in which a handful of political, economic, and military elites in western countries—especially the US—use violence and economic sanctions to jockey with non-western elites for greater control over the earth's natural resources, Assange suggests that the censorship is used primarily to reinforce existing imperial power relations. By resisting or abolishing censorship, he and other cypherpunks conclude that we can undermine imperial power relations and promote regional self-determination and free individual expression.

The cypherpunk vision of a censorship-free world may seem utopian, but they remind us that censorship itself is riddled with dangers other than the mere restriction of information. For one thing, censorship cannot be enforced without mass surveillance, which means that censorship not only deprives individuals of knowledge and speech but also threatens privacy for the weak. As Assange notes:

> in order to have internet censorship there must also be internet surveillance. In order to check what someone is looking at, to see whether it is permitted or denied, [the authorities] must be seeing it, and therefore if [they] are seeing it [they] can record it all.
> (Assange et al. 2012, 114)

Anticipating counterarguments that there are certain kinds of information that most people agree should be restricted, Assange argues that censorship targeting even one kind of information cannot be effective without mass surveillance of some kind. Without "a technical architecture to do the censorship," censorship becomes impossible (Assange et al. 2012, 124).

However, even though we usually think of censorship as overt, explicit restrictions on information, Assange argues that censorship is often more subtle, implied, and informal, especially in western countries where so-called free speech is protected. To illustrate his point, Assange argues that censorship is less like a one-dimensional policy and more like a pyramid with several layers (Figure 7.1). The first layer of censorship—the tip of the pyramid and the most publicly visible form of censorship—consists of overt censorship practices, such as libel suits against publishers, the confiscation of journalists' documents or devices, and the assassination of journalists. The second layer is self-censorship practiced by those who want to avoid being subjected to the censorship methods in the first layer. The third layer consists of writing paid for by the subject of the piece, as is the case with "native advertisements." The fourth layer consists of all writing that is generally considered marketable to specific audiences. The fifth layer includes unequal access to education and disparities in literacy, which place limits on people's ability to understand information when it is available. The final layer consists in the limitations of information distribution, including the barriers of natural language and transition and the practice of placing information behind paywalls (Assange et al. 2012, 121–122; Assange 2016, 71–72). Only the first layer of censorship is explicitly visible to the public; the other layers are buried under "complexity and secrecy" (Assange et al. 2012, 122). Understanding censorship in this way, Assange argues that there are many barriers to the free circulation of information.

Censorship is about information, which means that censorship is about power, but crypto can help redistribute power on the individual and organizational levels, and this includes cases of censorship. Because crypto enables private communication, it also enables individuals to speak without being observed by surveillance powers. Because such speech cannot be observed, it cannot be censored. Tim May (2001b) states it plainly: "Strong crypto provides a technological means of ensuring the practical freedom to read and write what one wishes to" (77). For Assange, the issue of censorship comes down to the nature of personal efficacy in the digital age. Censorship restricts the freedom of public information, and when information is restricted, so is our ability to read, speak, and—most importantly—think. Assange tells us that we must make a choice: either we have to be willing to be careful about what we read and say so we do not get in trouble with

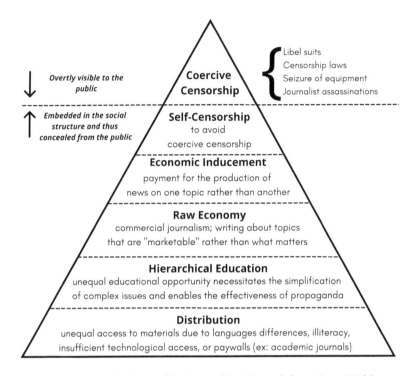

Figure 7.1 Assange's Censorship Pyramid. Adapted from Pope-Weideman (2013).

the authorities, or we need to master crypto technologies so we can communicate freely. "If people don't take that second step," Assange warns, "then we'll have a universal political correctness, because even when people are communicating with their closest friends they will be self-censors and will remove themselves as political actors from the world" (Assange et al. 2012, 62–63). On this view, crypto helps liberate our thinking from the watchful eyes of the censors, technologically shielding the information we access and the thoughts we express from surveillance.

On the institutional level, crypto can help small, relatively powerless organizations circumvent censorship, and WikiLeaks is a paradigm example. To protect WikiLeaks against censorship attempts, Assange (2016) built the site with two features: hidden servers accessible only through Tor and a distributed front. When visiting most websites, your computer connects directly to the server cluster that hosts the site's content, but when connecting to WikiLeaks, which uses a hidden server, your computer connects to a server that presents the content but not the server where the content is in fact stored. Because WikiLeaks' hidden server is channeled through Tor, it is nearly impossible for attackers to discover the site's originating server. Likewise, WikiLeaks' distributed front includes many copies of the website we see when we visit it; whenever an attacker takes down "wikileaks.org," another copy of the site can go up in a matter of minutes. Though many powerful people would like to take WikiLeaks offline and prevent global publics from being able to read its publications, the site was purposefully constructed to be essentially censorship-proof. By using crypto, WikiLeaks can defend the privacy of a weak organization (and its whistleblower sources) while continuing to impose transparency on the powerful—and all of this circumvents censorship and thus advances the notion that all public information should be free.

On "Intellectual Property"

Steven Levy (2010) notes that although the original hackers "believed that property rights were nonexistent" (98), many of them nevertheless abandoned this belief once they began computer businesses. "As major shareholders of companies supporting hundreds of employees, the hackers found things not so simple," he writes (276). Lamenting the fact that "business interests have intruded on a culture that built on the ideals of openness and creativity" (470), Levy observes that "all of a sudden, they had secrets to keep" (276). The primary concern of the hacker-turned-entrepreneur was preventing members of the public from freely making copies of computer code. The hacker perspective insisted that code should be shared freely; the business perspective insisted that every person pay for their own copy. Thus, we have the dilemma of information in the digital age. As Stewart Brand so famously put it: "On the one hand, information wants to be expensive, because it is so valuable...On the other hand, information wants to be free, because the cost of getting it out is getting lower and lower all the time. So you have these two [tendencies] fighting against each other" (quoted in Turner 2006, 136). The hackers entering the business world abandoned their commitment to "all information should be free" and adopted a new motto: all information should be purchased.

The term "intellectual property" is an artful term of propaganda, for it obscures three important aspects about the legal controls over the distribution of ideas and information. First, "intellectual property" wrongly suggests that our notion of property in physical objects, such as land, cars, and toothbrushes, can and should be applied un-problematically to non-physical objects like ideas or information. Second, "intellectual property" is used as a catch-all term in place of the actual legal categories of copyright and patent (among others). While these are complicated areas of law, it is possible to get a general sense of their differences in the US context. A *copyright* provides the author of original works rendered into a tangible medium the right to control the reproduction, modification, and distribution of the work. A *patent* provides the inventor of a new and useful process or machine 20 years of exclusive rights to make and sell the process or machine. Third, "intellectual property" suggests that the purpose of these legal categories is to protect the "rights" of the creator or distributor rather than advance the public good. The term "intellectual property," then, seems designed to intentionally obfuscate the reality of legal controls over the distribution of ideas and information. As Richard Stallman (2005) states bluntly, "anyone using the term 'intellectual property' is typically either confused himself, or trying to confuse you."

To understand the ethical problems with so-called intellectual property, we must place copyright and patent law in their historical contexts. Cyberculture intellectual and cypherpunk fellow-traveler John Perry Barlow (1996) has challenged the first and third "intellectual property" obfuscations explained above, arguing that copyright and patent law were originally designed to promote "the free exchange of ideas." As Barlow explains, copyrights and patents were intended to bring the interests of authors and inventors into harmony with the interest of the public. An author might create new ideas or an engineer might invent a new machine, but if they keep these discoveries and creations to themselves, then the public will not benefit from them. So, copyrights and patents were offered to incentivize creators to share their ideas and machines with the world. The aim was not to protect the rights of the creators but to uplift humanity through the circulation of information. To receive copyrights and patent protection, the author or inventor was required to render their creations into physical, material form: a printed book or a workable machine, for instance. Once someone purchases a book or machine, that person *owns* the object; they can sell it, trade it, or gift it as they please because it is the object and not the ideas it contains or the design it embodies that is considered property.

In the digital age, however, authors write and share ideas, and inventors create and share code without rendering their creations into physical, material form. Digital creations simply consist of a flow of electrons rendered into ones and zeros. "Since it is now possible to convey ideas from one mind to another without ever making them physical," Barlow (1996) complains, "we are now claiming to own ideas themselves and not merely their expression" (15). This slight-of-hand, however, which conflates ownership of physical property with ideas, undermines the central purpose of copyright and patent law. Physical property makes sense because physical objects derive their value from scarcity, Barlow explains, but when this conception of value is applied to information, then copyright and patent law become means of creating artificial scarcity in information, thus impeding "the free exchange of ideas" and harming the public. "If we continue to assume that value is based on scarcity, as it is with regard to physical objects," Barlow warns, "we will create laws that are precisely contrary to the nature of information, which may, in many cases, increase in value with distribution" (17).

Barlow's worries about the harmful effects of copyright and patent law seem to have manifested in our modern political economy of information. As Jared Ball (2011) finds, the legal restrictions on "intellectual property" in the US have produced "a corporate monopoly over the rights to cultural expression and ultimately a state of 'corporate welfare' that has resulted in a decrease in the amount of artistic creation available to the public" (83). Notice that Ball does not say that fewer artistic creations are being produced; he only says that fewer are available for the public. In this twenty-first-century, post-industrial information economy, information creates more wealth and has a larger market share than airlines, automobiles, and agriculture, but most intellectual creations are owned and controlled by corporations, not individual authors, artists, and inventors. These corporations maintain their dominance on culture by using copyrights, patents, and licensing to control the circulation of information (82–85). Thus, as Barlow predicted, corporations use the very laws originally intended to promote "the free exchange of ideas" to create an artificial scarcity of cultural productions under their control. Those who challenge corporate power by circumventing the information controls imposed by copyright and patent law are of course subjected to legal, financial, and even penal punishment.

Most cypherpunks have only contempt for so-called intellectual property, for it creates a regime of censorship and impeded the hacker call for the freedom of all public information. As with any type of censorship, "intellectual property" restrictions are ineffective without mass surveillance. The US government has already enacted the Digital Millennium Copyright Act (DMCA), which imposes many restrictions on the freedom of information, but the cypherpunks have joined the international fight against other US-led initiatives to control "intellectual property" globally, including the somewhat successful campaigns against the Stop Online Piracy Act (SOPA) and the Protect Intellectual Property Act (PIPA), both of which were designed to give US agencies global authority in policing "intellectual property" violations (Assange et al. 2012). One recent threat to information freedom was the Anti-Counterfeit and Trade Agreement (ACTA), an international treaty negotiated in secret and to be used by powerful nations against weaker nations. Putting the issue terms that most cypherpunks would appreciate, one observer noted:

> The copyright oligopoly's real desire is to create an international *police state* dedicated to the protection of their rights…The proposed ACTA treaty would create international legislation turning *border guards* into copyright police, charged with checking laptops, iPods, and other devices for possibly infringing content, and given the authority to confiscate and destroy equipment without even requiring a complaint from a rights-holder.
>
> (quoted in Ball 2011, 85)

As the cypherpunks warn, treaties and laws like ACTA are intended to give imperial states like the US government legal authority to conduct mass surveillance in the serve of finding and punishing people who violate copyright law.

Like any policy that involves mass surveillance, cypherpunks insist upon the use of crypto in the circumvention of legal restrictions on information. "What was previously considered a common human resource, distributed among the minds and libraries of the world," Barlow (1996) writes, "is now being fenced and deeded" (15). In what almost seems like a direct reply, Tim May (2001b) responds: "the seemingly minor discovery out of an arcane branch of mathematics [will] come to be the wire clippers which dismantle the barbed wire around intellectual property" (63). By encrypting our communications, it becomes almost impossible for any surveillance apparatus to know whether we are coordinating dinner plans or sharing entire libraries of human knowledge. Thus, hackers and cypherpunks uncorrupted by business interests continue to uphold axiom that all public information should be free. Once again, Levy (2010) provides a helpful reminder that

> hackers believed people should be allowed to access files or tools which might promote the hacker quest to find out and improve the

way the world works. When a hacker needed something to help him create, explore, or fix, he did not bother with such ridiculous concepts as property rights.

(95)

On Free Software and Open Access

The *New York Times'* first mention of Julian Assange was in March 2001, over five years before he founded WikiLeaks (Dembart 2001). The article, "The End User: Text for the Taking," reported that there were an increasing number of websites providing free digital access to books out of copyright. "In addition," the author noted, "there are some new books, still in copyright, whose authors and publishers have decided to give them away." The example: *Underground* by Suelette Dreyfus and Julian Assange, published by Random House in 1997. Dreyfus explained that she and her coauthor were giving away unlimited copies of their book

> because part of the joy of creating a piece of art is in knowing that many people can be—and are—enjoying it. Particularly people who can't otherwise afford to pay $11 for a book. People such as cash-strapped hackers.

Lest the critics accuse the cypherpunks of hypocrisy, demanding free materials from other while closely guarding their own intellectual productions, we must realize that cypherpunks put their principles into practice. Dreyfus and Assange's decision should come as no surprise, for in "A Cypherpunk's Manifesto," Eric Hughes (2001) states unequivocally that "Our code is free for all to use, worldwide" (82–83). Though cypherpunks need income like anyone else, they refuse to call upon the coercive power of the state to penalize anyone who accesses their intellectual creations without permission or payment.

Cypherpunks and hackers look to create alternatives to the "intellectual property" machine, and two of the most illustrative attempts to do so are the free software and open access movements. Led by the computer scientist Richard M. Stallman, the free software movement calls for and works to create computer programs that are liberated from copyright and licensing restrictions. Back in 1983, when many hackers were being seduced by business interests and abandoning their commitment to information freedom, Stallman was a holdout, earning him the title "last of the true hackers" (Levy 2010). For Stallman

(2021), *free* software is not software that is given away without charging money, though many free software projects are, in fact, cost-free in this sense. Instead, *free* software means software that is free from legal controls over who can read, modify, and share the software, hence the term "liberated." As Stallman insists, we must think of "free speech" not "free beer." "Many of the cypherpunks were closely involved in the free/open source software movement," Finn Brunton (2019) observes, "which took as a fundamental aim that software must necessarily be open—available for review, study, sharing, debugging, and improvement" (93). The cypherpunks' desire to share code and promote convivial tools resonates closely with Stallman's free software project.

To best understand this movement, it is important to distinguish between three categories: proprietary software, open source software, and free software. *Proprietary* software are programs for which users cannot access or read the source code and which cannot be altered, copied, and/or distributed without violating copyright and licensing restrictions. For Stallman, such software is unfree, and it imposes an unequal and unjust power relationship between the copyright holder and the user. Furthermore, proprietary software should often be considered malware. Because users cannot inspect the source code, proprietary software can contain back doors (enabling unauthorized remote control of data or computer functions), digital restrictions management (DRM imposes data controls, such as prevention of file copying), jailing (systems that prevent users from running "unapproved" programs), and tethers (requiring a remote server connection for full program functionality) ("Proprietary" 2021). *Open source* software, which allows users to access and read a program's source code, is somewhat better than proprietary software, but Stallman (2021) insists that it should not be confused with free software because most open source programs are still subject to various degrees of licensing restriction. So even though users can "look at the code" of open source software, such software is not liberated from legal restrictions on modification and distribution of the code.

Free software is, by contrast, free of copyright and licensing restrictions. As the "Philosophy of the GNU Project" states, free software respects the user's "four essential freedoms": "(0) to run the program, (1) to study and change the program in source code form, (2) to redistribute exact copies, and (3) to distribute modified versions." Like open source software, free software allows users to access and read the source code, but unlike open source software, free software also allows, in *every* instance, users to distribute unmodified copies of the program, change the program for personal use, and distribute modifications of the program. Thus, free software embodies the original hacker ethic, which held that, "instead of everybody writing his own version of the same program, the best version would be available to everyone, and everyone would be free to delve into the code and improve on *that*" (Levy 2010, 29). It should come as no surprise that cypherpunks support such practices. As Jacob Appelbaum argues:

> We need free software for a free world...We need software that is as free as laws in a democracy, where everyone is able to study it, to change it, to be able to really understand it and to ensure that it does what they wish that it would do.
>
> (Assange et al. 2012, 150–151)

In addition to supporting free software, cypherpunks also support open access. In its mainstream iterations, the open access movement seeks to make academic and scientific research available without cost to the reader, allowing anyone in the global reading public to benefit from the production of scholarship. As Peter Suber (2015) explains, the primary concern of open access publishing is to eliminate cost barriers to scientific knowledge. However, many in the open access movement have also pushed to eliminate various levels of licensing restrictions. Some open access publications can be downloaded and freely modified and shared among peers, while others can be freely downloaded but impose limitations on users' ability to distribute derivative products. In this sense, some open access material is analogous to free software, while other open access material is analogous to open source software. Open access advocates recognize that open access does not mean universal access, for like the lower layers of Assange's censorship pyramid, internet connectivity, language barriers, literacy rates, and other impediments outside the publisher's control may still limit user access. The mainstream open access movement is somewhat conservative when it comes to information freedom, for it argues that open access is compatible with copyright law. Most materials that are published open access are either older texts for which the copyright has expired (public domain material) or new texts for which the legally recognized copyright holder has authorized open, payment-free distribution of their work.

For hackers committed to the axiom that all public information should be free, the mainstream open access movement does not do enough, and though many have pushed the movement to do more, one intellectual stands out: Aaron Swartz. In his "Guerilla Open Access Manifesto," Swartz (2008) argues that it is unjust to allow corporations to charge fees for the world's scientific research, copyrights or not. "The world's entire scientific and cultural heritage, published over centuries in books and journals, is increasingly being digitized and locked up by a handful of private corporations," Swartz explains. He argues that it is not enough to focus solely on public domain materials and new or forthcoming scholarship, as the mainstream open access movement does. By using copyright to restrict the freedom of scientific knowledge, politicians and corporations have conspired in the "private theft of public culture." Swartz argues that faculty, students, and anyone else with access to paywalled science and scholarship have a moral obligation to download articles and distribute them online, for "sharing isn't immoral—it's a moral imperative." Because "there is no justice in following unjust laws," Swartz calls for a mass campaign of civil disobedience. "We need to take information, wherever it is stored, make our copies and share them with the world," he insists.

> We need to take stuff that's out of copyright and add it to the archive. We need to buy secret databases and put them on the Web. We need to download scientific journals and upload them to file sharing networks. We need to fight for Guerilla Open Access.

Swartz called for Guerilla Open Access; he also practiced it. In 2008, Swartz used software to download 2.7 million documents from the Public Access to Court Electronic Records (PACER), the US federal judiciary's paywalled website for public access to court records. Even though those court files were and are public documents without copyright restrictions, and even though digital data storage and transmission has become increasingly easy and inexpensive, PACER charged members of the public seven to ten cents per page to download the documents, netting the website approximately $100 million beyond operating costs. Because the documents were public and because Swartz had not violated any of PACER's largely nonexistent terms of service, he was not prosecuted. However, the documents revealed systemic privacy issues in the way court documents were filed, and Swartz used the events to push for privacy reforms and for a more open PACER system (Lee 2013). From September 2010 to January 2011, Swartz again used a program to download what is estimated to be millions of academic articles from the database JSTOR. Originally, Swartz accessed the articles through the open wireless network on Massachusetts Institute of Technology's (MIT) campus, but his IP address was blocked after JSTOR and MIT detected thousands of requests coming from his computer. Swartz found an unlocked closet and connected his laptop directly to the network, leaving it there to download articles. When his laptop was discovered, MIT and the US Secret Service set up a sting operation, catching Swartz when he returned for his computer. He never posted the downloaded articles online, but prosecutors used the "Guerilla Open Access Manifesto" as evidence that Swartz *intended* to share the article in violation of copyright law. Swartz returned the files to JSTOR, which decided not to press charges. Nevertheless, MIT and federal prosecutors indicted Swartz on 13 felony charges, threatening him with up to 35 years in prison (Hsieh 2013). Caught up in the Obama administration's fanatical crackdown on "hackers" (Fakhoury 2014) and "leakers" (Gardner 2016), Swartz committed suicide in January 2013 at the age of 26.

Hackers and cypherpunks have sought alternatives to the information-repressive restrictions of so-called intellectual property regimes, and the free software and open access movements are but two prominent examples of such alternatives. Pushing for free, liberated software, as opposed to merely open source software, Stallman seeks to free computer code from copyrights and patents, allowing the inventions of programmers to engage in the ethical work of freeing the world's public information. Likewise, calling for more civil disobedience in the pursuit of open access scholarship and knowledge, Swartz forces us to reckon with the ethics of information control and information freedom. No one truly knows what Swartz intended to do with the documents he downloaded at MIT, but the fact that he was at MIT when he did it brings us somewhat full circle. In his pioneering book on hacker culture, Levy (2010) traces the origins of the hacker ethic to MIT in 1959. The notion that all information should be free was born at MIT. "In the monastic confines of the Massachusetts Institute of Technology," Levy writes, "people had the freedom to live out this dream—the hacker dream" (38). When MIT and the US government persecuted Swartz using the most punitive measures possible, they not only killed the hacker dream, they killed a hacker. By locking the world's public information behind "intellectual property" restrictions and then policing those locks with military force, governments and corporations seek to transform the hacker dream into a hacker nightmare.

Conclusion

Hacker culture and cypherpunks ethics are not synonymous, but they do share some key commitments, the most important of which is the belief that all public information should be free. Censorship deprives individuals, communities, and humanity from the opportunity for the greatest possible enrichment and advancement. Copyrights, patents, and other so-called intellectual property laws impose undue censorship on public information, and like all forms of censorship, "intellectual property" violations cannot be policed effectively without mass surveillance capabilities. As we saw in previous chapters, mass surveillance is an existential threat to privacy for the weak, which means that protesting privacy and freeing information are intimately connected. Armed with crypto, we can defend privacy, and armed with privacy, we can freely circulate information. It should come as no surprise, therefore, that the same governments and corporations that oppose the availability of strong crypto also oppose the free circulation of public information. While corporations use copyrights to police the circulation of code and patents to restrict the development of code, free software allows us to circumvent these restrictions, putting convivial tools back in the hands of the public and thus increasing everyone's autonomy. Likewise, as information becomes more valuable and thus subjected to artificial scarcity under law, open access practices—whether moderate or guerilla—can help us bring science out from behind corporate paywalls and into the public.

The freedom of information is not just a hacker principle; it is an idea embedded in digital communication networks. As Levy (2010) writes, ARPAnet, the precursor to what we now call the internet, embodied "the belief that systems should be decentralized, encourage exploration, and urge a free flow of information" (138). The internet is no different. As Zimmermann compellingly argues:

> a free, open and universal internet is probably the most important tool that we have to address the global issues that are at stake, that protecting it is probably one of the most essential tasks that our generation has between its hands, and that when somebody somewhere—whether it's a government or a company—restricts some people's ability to access the universal internet, it is the whole internet that is affected. It's the whole of humanity that is being restricted…It's about sharing that knowledge freely and enabling communication channels for knowledge to flow freely…we embed that notion of freedom in the way we build alternatives and build technology and build models.
>
> (Assange et al. 2012, 148, 152)

Situating the notion of information freedom within cypherpunk ethics more broadly, crypto anarchy and crypto justice seem to have somewhat different ideas about the principle all public information should be free. Tim May, who has no roots in the hacker underground of the 1980s, is not exactly clear where he stands on information freedom. On the one hand, May (2001a, 2001b) believes that it is a *fact* that crypto will undermine the ability of corporations to control knowledge, but it is not clear whether he believes that we *ought* to use crypto for such purposes. On the other hand, as an anarcho-capitalist with a strong belief in individual property rights, May (2001a, 2001c, 73) sometimes suggests that authors and other creators ought to get their "proper cut of the action" (35). Importantly, information freedom is not incompatible with the practice of paying people for use of their creations, but it does require us to change our vision of what payment means and how it is handled. For his own part, Assange (2011) is unequivocal. "We have an innate aversion to censorship," he writes, "and the Web can speak to that" (119) because "the Internet is, by its true nature, a censorship-free zone," he writes (104). Thus, while May's writings do not give us a clear image of where he stands on information freedom, Assange argues that justice cannot be realized without making all public information free.

8   Conclusion

A Tale of Two Cryptographers

Between March and June 2013, Arvind Narayanan published a short, two-part article titled "What happened to the crypto dream?" in the journal *IEEE Security and Privacy*. In a somewhat smug, condescending analysis, Narayanan (2013b) argues that crypto has done little to protect privacy and that this was largely because of the cypherpunks. He organizes crypto into two basic types: *cypherpunk crypto*, built upon "the dream of wielding crypto as a weapon for social and political change," and *pragmatic crypto*, "a more down-to-earth view that seeks to engineer modest privacy enhancements in specific applications" (68). For Narayanan (2013a), cypherpunk crypto never took off because there is no public interest in using crypto for social change. Citizens in "democratic countries" have little need for encrypted communications, and most members of the public prefer traditional, easy-to-use fiat currency over complicated cryptocurrencies. He dismisses claims that Bitcoin and WikiLeaks represent a revival of cypherpunk crypto, saying that the former had "essentially no societal impact" (except for Silk Road users) and the latter was, like Cryptome, "a far cry from cypherpunk rhetoric" (76). According to Narayanan, cypherpunk crypto is impractical and should be abandoned.

Following his call to give up the rhetoric of cypherpunk crypto, Narayanan (2013b) recommends a pragmatic crypto approach focusing on refining consumer choice in the tech market through the incremental development of privacy applications. Narayanan asserts, without evidence or citations, that "Consumers don't seek technological privacy protection against governments and service providers but against their peers, nosy neighbors, stalkers, employers, insurance companies, advertisers, and the like" (70). Tellingly, Narayanan's

DOI: 10.4324/9781003220534-8

subjects are "consumers"—not citizens, not human beings. Even if people did seek privacy from their service providers:

> Hardware and software are increasingly vertically integrated and packed together in a way that users can't fully control or modify. This is reinforced by legal restrictions such as the Digital Millennium Copyright Act. Combined with the fact that today's software typically updates automatically, not trusting vendors isn't an option anymore.
>
> (70)

According to Narayanan, then, most *consumers* trust their service providers, but their preferences matter little because "intellectual property" laws like the DMCA give them no choice.

Readers of this book will see that Narayanan knows almost nothing about the cypherpunks; he discusses so many cypherpunk creations but fails to grasp their intellectual and historical connections. Readers will likewise see that Narayanan's proposal for pragmatic crypto is, in the terminology of Ivan Illich, *manipulative* rather than *convivial*. Humans are reduced to consumers and then given no choice but to trust the largest, richest, most powerful, and most unaccountable economic organizations in the history of our species. Narayanan's naive arguments barely had time to propagate, for the month after Part 2 of his essay appeared, Edward Snowden revealed to the world that the "democratic" US government was engaged in a nationwide—nay, planetary—mass surveillance operation and that these so-called trustworthy "service providers" and "vendors" were willing, active partners in that mass surveillance. Of course, the cypherpunks had long warned of a transnational mass surveillance dystopia maintained through the coordination of corporations and democratically unaccountable intelligence agencies, but instead of studying the cypherpunks, Narayanan simply makes a few factually and conceptually errant observations about the movement before dismissing them entirely.

A different approach to the cypherpunks can be found in Phillip Rogaway's (2015) "The Moral Character of Cryptographic Work." As both a person and a professional cryptographer, Rogaway was deeply influenced by the Snowden revelations of mass surveillance. As a result, he calls for greater political and ethical awareness on the part of academics and scientists, arguing that cypherpunks have a lot to offer in this area. As Rogaway says about cypherpunk ethics:

> When I first encountered such discourse, I smugly thought the authors were way over-promising: they needed to tone down this

rhetoric to be accurate. I no longer think this way. More engaged in implementing systems than I'll ever be, top cypherpunks understand more than I about insecure operating systems, malware, programming bugs, subversion, side channels, poor usability, small anonymity sets, and so on. Cypherpunks believe that *despite* such obstacles, cryptography can *still* be transformative.

(18)

Unlike Narayanan, who dismisses the cypherpunks with an arrogance so common in the academy (in articles locked behind a paywall), Rogaway approached the cypherpunks with humility, openness, a desire to learn (in a paper freely available online). Rogaway came away realizing that he could indeed learn from them. He was willing to *listen*. Rogaway's experience with the writings and creations of the cypherpunks is like my own experience with them. Though I am a philosopher and he is a cryptographer, we both found something of value in the movement.

I have written this book in a way that highlights what I have learned from the cypherpunks. The sparse existing scholarship on the cypherpunks—nearly all of which is abhorrent—tries too hard to cram the cypherpunks into existing academic theories of so-called hackers, hacktivists, anarchists, and so on. Very few academics respect the cypherpunks enough to study them carefully, and even fewer believe that they have anything to learn from the movement. I have taken a different approach. While I have coined new terms, referred to academic publications, and appealed to philosophical texts, I have done so only to elucidate and organize, to the best of my ability, the cypherpunks' own philosophies. What I have said and how I have said it will necessarily inform and shape the reader's perspective on the cypherpunks—there is no replacement for reading the primary texts, after all—but I have tried my best to give a platform to their ideas, even when it comes to ideas with which I personally disagree. Most importantly, I hope this disposition has rubbed off on the reader.

In the famous opening sentence of *A Tale of Two Cities*—"It was the best of times, it was the worst of times"—Charles Dickens presents the reader with a bifurcated world, a world balanced on the fragile fulcrum between wisdom and foolishness, belief and incredulity, light and darkness, hope and despair, everything and nothing. Whether we consider the writings of the crypto anarchists of the 1990s or the writings of contemporary cypherpunks like Assange, we get a similar description, imagery of a world bursting with the potential for total global authoritarianism or the potential for complete global emancipation. While this may at first appear to be nothing more than a hyperbolic false dichotomy, the debate between Narayanan and Rogaway suggests that there is more than a kernel of truth to the cypherpunks' claims. While Narayanan seems resigned to the emerging world of foolishness, incredulity, darkness, and despair, Rogaway argues that it is still possible to fight for a world of wisdom, belief, light, and hope. To be completely honest, I am utterly pessimistic. However, if there is to be any hope, then we need to build convivial tools for a convivial future.

Toward a Convivial Future

The first aim of this book is conceptual. I wanted to introduce and substantiate "two important distinctions so that future studies of the cypherpunks can approach this subject in a better, more refined manner. First, by differentiating cypherpunks as a movement distinct from "hackers" and "cyberpunks," I hope future studies will resist the temptation to collapse cypherpunks into other categories. Second, by highlighting the deep philosophical differences between May's crypto anarchy and Assange's "crypto justice," I hope to banish from all future commentary on the cypherpunks and WikiLeaks, academic or otherwise, the suggestion that Assange is a crypto anarchist. The ongoing tendency to obfuscate these distinctions rather than pursue them reflects poorly on scholars; such laziness has caused many important and interesting features of the cypherpunk movement to go unnoticed and unappreciated. The distinctions introduced in the book provide a roadmap for future scholarship, but they also demonstrate how insipid it is for people in the US to interpret Assange and his work at WikiLeaks through the narrow confines of nationalist politics and partisan affiliation. Those who to cram WikiLeaks into a Democrat versus Republican paradigm reveal more about the limitations of their own thinking than they do about Assange's political and journalistic project. Because these partisan myrmidons cannot be bothered to think beyond the comfortable boundaries of party and country, they contribute daily to Assange's death.

The second aim of this book is political. By introducing and exploring cypherpunk principles like *privacy for the weak*, *transparency for the powerful*, and *all public information should to be free*, I hope to stimulate readers into new ways of thinking about information circulation and communication systems. There are, of course, the inane retorts that people trot out as if they are original—"Hey, I have nothing to hide," "Governments have secrets for a reason," "Artists have to eat, too, you know." I have found that when people are pushed to explain these statements, they either don't really believe them, or they have no evidence-based arguments to support them. Instead, these retorts work as a kind of rhetorical patchwork for misguided, misinformed understandings of the world. The digital world is so complex that few of us truly understand it. While most individual people struggle to understand the complex structure of the digital world, government and corporations have a thorough understanding of the digital world *because they built it and they control it.* Governments and corporations use this strategic position of control to their advantage: they built systems so they can know more and more about you and while you know less and less about them. Google and Facebook track everything you do and say. As a result, they make billions of dollars (power), control massive collections of behavioral data (power), and coordinate with government to protect their interests (power)—you get "relevant" advertisements. By demanding that all public information be free, we can better learn how these systems work, and by practicing privacy for the weak and transparency for the powerful, we can each do our small part in shifting the balance of power away from powerful organizations and toward individuals and local communities.

The third aim of this book is practical, and it relates to technology in two ways. First, I wanted to make a small contribution to the demystification of crypto for those in the humanities and social sciences. When I began my research on the cypherpunks, I had no clue how crypto works. I watched videos, reviewed diagrams, and read explanations, but it was not until I started studying the technical aspects of crypto that I truly appreciated the features that make it work. Now that I know a little more about the crypto, I understand the limitations of all the videos and diagrams I relied on before. On this point, Rogaway (2015) makes a relevant observation: "Cryptography is serious, with ideas often hard to understand. When we try to explain them with cartoons and cute narratives, I don't think we make our contributions easier to understand. What we actually do is add in a layer of obfuscation that must be peeled away to understand what has actually been done" (37). We should not treat technical knowledge as mysterious; we should treat it as something to learn. There is a difference between saying, "I *don't* understand it" and "I *can't* understand it." When we say "I *don't* understand it," we are describing our current state of knowledge. When we say "I *can't* understand it," we are giving an excuse for not trying. I do not mean that understanding the technical aspects of crypto is easy, but I do mean that we should not give up before we have started.

Second, I wanted to help readers think about not just crypto but all technology. Following Ivan Illich's distinction between manipulative (or industrial) tools and convivial tools, I argue that we ought to examine every piece of technology we encounter to see if it promotes the autonomy of individuals and local communities (convivial) or if it undermines such autonomy (manipulative). My approach is justified by the history of computing. Lee Felsenstein, an original participant in the computer hobbyist movement of the 1970s and designer of the Osborne 1, the first mass-produced portable computer, read Illich's *Tools for Conviviality* in the 1970s and began working to bring convivial computers out of the universities and into the public. As Levy (2010) reports, Felsenstein "was part of a collective effort to take the first few steps in a momentous battle that the MIT hackers had never considered worth fighting: to spread the Hacker Ethic by bringing computers to the people" (154). Felsenstein was an ardent critic of the emerging big tech industry. As hackers gave up on the hacker ethic and became part of the corporate directorate, they began designing and selling manipulative computers rather than convivial ones. In 1975, Felsenstein gave a conference talk indicting the nascent tech industry:

> The industrial [manipulative] approach is grim and doesn't work: the design motto is "Design by Geniuses for Use by Idiots," and the watchword for dealing with the untrained and unwashed public is *keep their hands off!*...The convivial approach I suggest would rely on the user's ability to learn about and gain some control over the tool. The user will have to spend some amount of time probing around inside the equipment, and we will have to make this possible and not fatal to either the equipment or the person.
>
> (Levy 2010, 242)

Felsenstein's comments reveal that the digital age was fraught with a tension between the manipulative and the convivial *from the beginning.* And Narayanan's comments about vertical integration and laws like the DMCA suggest that the manipulative has prevailed.

To turn the world around, putting it on a path toward conviviality rather than manipulation, we need more than crypto and cypherpunks ethics. But crypto offers itself as a useful tool and cypherpunks ethics provide a useful conceptual starting point. Cypherpunks want to build a convivial future. As Assange himself insists:

> we can, in fact, must build the tools of a new democracy. We can actually build them with our minds, distribute them to other people and engage in collective defense. Technology and science [are] not neutral. There are particular forms of technology that can give

us these fundamental rights and freedoms that many people have
aspired to for so long.

(Assange et al. 2012, 149)

To be sure, building such a future will not be easy. As the lives of many
people discussed in this book reveal, those who challenge the powerful will be found, they will be fixed, and they will be finished. Learning about, developing, and using crypto is enough to make someone
a target of institutions like the NSA, and when someone uses crypto
to challenge power more broadly, they find themselves targeted by
the rest of the power apparatus. More importantly, convivial uses of
crypto need not lead to one, homogenous future for us all—quite the
opposite. As Assange argues, "you can build a wide variety of political
systems" using crypto, and this is a good thing. "Utopia to me would
be a dystopia if there was just one," he adds. "Utopian ideals must
mean the diversity of systems and models of interaction" (Assange
et al. 2012, 156). Though cypherpunks like May and Assange have
ideas about what kinds of societies they would like to create, we need
not conform our hopes to theirs. Instead, we should consider all the
different kinds of societies that crypto can help us built and then we
should build them.

When Ron Rivest, Adi Shamir, and Leonard Adleman wrote their
groundbreaking paper on public key crypto, the NSA scrambled to
suppress the paper, arguing that it was a crime to distribute crypto
research. Computer scientist Mark Miller managed to get a pre-
publication copy of the RSA paper. Miller believed that the NSA was
going to classify the RSA paper and prevent it from seeing the light of
day, so he made a hundred photocopies and sent them to magazines,
organizations, and colleagues. His message: "If I disappear, make sure
this gets out" ("Cypherpunks" 2021, 21:23). With good reason, Miller
was worried that the NSA was going to lock up one of the most important scientific discoveries of the twentieth century, but he feared
that his efforts to prevent the NSA from doing so would make him a
target. I do not believe that having merely written this book makes me
a target, and I do not believe that simply reading this book makes you
a target. I do however want to end this book with a message similar to
Miller's: Whether or not I disappear, *make sure this gets out.*

References

Addley, Esther. 2014. "Julian Assange Has Had His Human Rights Violated, Says Ecuador Foreign Minister." *The Guardian*, August 18, 2014. https://archive.md/wraYU.

Amoore, Louise, and Marieke De Goede. 2005. "Governance, Risk, and Dataveillance in the War on Terror." *Crime Law & Social Change* 43: 149–173.

Anderson, Patrick D. 2021. "Privacy for the Weak, Transparency for the Powerful: The Cypherpunk Ethics of Julian Assange." *Ethics and Information Technology* 23, no. 3: 295–308.

Androutsellis-Theotokis, Stephanos, and Diomidis Spinellis. 2004. "A Survey of Peer-to-Peer Content Distribution Technologies." *ACM Computing Surveys* 36, no. 4: 335–371.

Aristotle. 1999. *Nicomachean Ethics*. Second Edition. Translated and edited by Terence Irwin. Indianapolis: Hackett Publishing Company.

Assange, Julian. 2006. "Conspiracy as Governance." *Cryptome* (blog), December 3, 2006. http://archive.fo/kr8Pr.

Assange, Julian. 2010. "Don't Shoot Messenger for Revealing Uncomfortable Truths." *The Australian*, December 7, 2010. http://archive.fo/SmXpG.

Assange, Julian. 2011. *Julian Assange: The Unauthorized Biography*. Edinburgh: Canongate Books.

Assange, Julian. 2013 "How Cryptography Is a Key Weapon in the Fight against Empire States." *The Guardian*, July 9, 2013: http://archive.ph/Mbsx4.

Assange, Julian. 2014. "Who Should Own the Internet?" *New York Times*, December 4, 2014: https://archive.fo/vxLJd.

Assange, Julian. 2015. "Introduction: WikiLeaks and Empire." In *The WikiLeaks Files: The World According to US Empire*, 1–19. New York: Verso.

Assange, Julian. 2016. *When Google Met WikiLeaks*. New York: OR Books.

Assange, Julian. 2017. Forward to *How I Lost by Hillary Clinton*. Edited by Joe Lauria. New York: OR Books.

Assange, Julian, Jacob Appelbaum, Andy Müller-Maguhn, and Jérémie Zimmermann. 2012. *Cypherpunks: Freedom and the Future of the Internet*. New York: OR Books.

Avila, Renata, Sarah Harrison, and Angela Richter. 2017. *Women, Whistleblowing, WikiLeaks: A Conversation.* New York: OR Books.

Bady, Aaron. 2010. "Julian Assange and the Computer Conspiracy: 'To Destroy This Invisible Government.'" *zunguzungu* (blog), November 29, 2010. https://archive.fo/4nIaQ.

Ball, Jared. 2011. *I Mix What I Like: A Mixtape Manifesto.* Oakland, CA: AK Press.

Bamford, James. 1982. *The Puzzle Palace: A Report on NSA, America's Most Secret Agency.* Boston: Houghton Mifflin.

Bamford, James. 2008. *The Shadow Factory: The Ultra-Secret NSA from 9/11 to the Eavesdropping on America.* New York: Doubleday.

Barlow, John Perry. 1996. "Selling Wine without Bottles: The Economy of Mind on the Global Net." In *High Noon on the Electronic Frontier: Conceptual Issues in Cyberspace.* Edited by Peter Ludlow, 9–34. Cambridge: The MIT Press.

Bearman, Joshua. 2015a. "The Untold Story of Silk Road, Part 1." *Wired,* May 2015. https://archive.md/W1RQi.

Bearman, Joshua. 2015b. "The Untold Story of Silk Road, Part 2: The Fall." *Wired,* June 2015. https://archive.md/cYv43.

Bell, Jim. 1997. "Assassination Politics." *Cryptome* (blog), April 3, 1997. https://cryptome.org/ap.htm.

Benkler, Yochai. 2011. "A Free Irresponsible Press: Wikileaks and the Battle over the Soul of the Networked Fourth Estate." *Harvard Civil Rights-Civil Liberties Law Review* 46: 311–397.

Blumenthal, Max. 2020. "'The American Friends': New Court Files Expose Sheldon Adelson's Security Team in US spy operation against Julian Assange." *The Greyzone,* May 14, 2020. https://archive.md/rezeG

Brin, David. 1998. *The Transparent Society: Will Technology Force us to Choose between Privacy and Freedom?* Reading, MA: Addison-Wesley.

Brunton, Finn. 2011. "Keyspace: WikiLeaks and the Assange Papers." *Radical Philosophy* 166: 8–20.

Brunton, Finn. 2019. *Digital Cash: The Unknown History of the Anarchists, Utopians, and Technologists who Built Cryptocurrency.* Princeton: Princeton University Press.

Burke, Colin. 2020. "Digital Sousveillance: A Network Analysis of the US Surveillant Assemblage." *Surveillance & Society* 18, no. 1: 74–89.

Burnham, David. 1983. *The Rise of the Computer State: The Threat to our Freedoms, Our Ethics, and Our Democratic Process.* New York: Open Road Distribution.

Carey, James. 2009. *Communication as Culture: Essays on Media and Society, Revised Edition.* New York: Routledge.

Carlin, George. 1998. *Brain Droppings.* New York: Hyperion.

Chaos Computer Club. n.d. "Hacker Ethics." *Chaos Computer Club.* https://archive.md/ujjnP.

Chaum, David. 1985. "Security without Identification: Transaction Systems to Make Big Brother Obsolete." *Communications of the ACM,* 28: 1030–1044.

Chen, Adrian. 2011. "The Underground Website Where You Can Buy Any Drug Imaginable." *Gawker*, June 1, 2011. https://archive.md/RIWDc.

Cleaver, Eldridge. 2006. *Target Zero: A Life in Writing*. Edited by Kathleen Cleaver. New York: Palgrave Macmillan.

Coleman, E. Gabriella, and Alex Golub. 2008. "Hacker Practice: Moral Genres and the Cultural Articulation of Liberalism." *Anthropological Theory* 8, no. 3: 255–277.

Crary, David. 2013. "Older, Quieter than WikiLeaks, Cryptome Perseveres." *Associated Press*, March 9, 2013. https://archive.md/NR1Ge.

"Cypherpunks Write Code." 2021. "ReasonTV." November 1, 2021. Documentary, 33:54. https://youtu.be/9vM0oIEhMag.

Daemen, Joan, and Vincent Rijmen. 1999. "The Rijndael Block Cipher: AES Proposal." Document Version 2, March 9, 1999. https://web.archive.org/web/20070203204845/https://csrc.nist.gov/CryptoToolkit/aes/rijndael/Rijndael.pdf.

de Lagasnerie, Geoffroy. 2019. "Julian Assange for the Future." In *Defense of Julian Assange*, edited by Tariq Ali and Margaret Kunstler, 244–250. New York: OR Books.

de Zwart, Melissa. 2016. "Privacy for the weak, transparency for the powerful." In *Comparative Defamation and Privacy Law*, edited by Andrew T. Kenyon, 224–245. Cambridge: Cambridge University Press.

Dembart, Lee. 2001. "The End User: Text for the Taking." *New York Times*, March 26, 2001. https://archive.vn/JOhuF.

Di Salvo, Philip. 2020. *Digital Whistleblowing Platforms in Journalism: Encrypting Leaks*. Cham: Palgrave Macmillan.

Diffie, Whitfield, and Martin Hellman. 1976. "New Directions in Cryptography." *IEEE Transactions on Information Theory* 22, no. 6: 644–654.

Dorfman, Zach, Sean D. Naylor, and Michael Isikoff. 2021. "Kidnapping, Assassination and a London Shoot-Out: Inside the CIA's Secret War Plans against WikiLeaks." *Yahoo! News*, September 26, 2021. https://archive.md/2sX3Q.

Dreyfus, Suelette, and Julian Assange. 2012. *Underground*. Edinburgh: Canongate Books.

Durant, Will, and Ariel Durant. 1967. *Rousseau and Revolution: A History of Civilization in France, England, and Germany from 1756, and in the Remainder of Europe from 1715, to 1789*. New York: MJF Books.

"English Letter Frequency (based on a sample of 40,000 words)." n.d. https://archive.md/m4HhG.

Epstein, Jim. 2018. "Tim May, Father of 'Crypto Anarchy,' Is Dead at 66." *Reason*, December 16, 2018. https://archive.md/pmpzS.

Fakhoury, Hanni. 2014. "The U.S. Crackdown on Hackers Is Our New War on Drugs." *Wired*, January 23, 2014. https://archive.md/AQDoL.

Friedman, David. 2014. *The Machinery of Freedom: Guide to a Radical Capitalism*. Third Edition. New York: David Friedman.

Gardner, Lloyd C. 2016. *The War on Leakers: National Security and American Democracy, from Eugene V. Debs to Edward Snowden*. New York: The New Press.

Garner, Richard T., and Bernard Rosen. 1967. *Moral Philosophy: A Systematic Introduction to Normative Ethics and Meta-Ethics.* New York: Macmillan.

Gilmore, John. 1991. "Privacy, Technology, and the Open Society." *Computer Professionals for Social Responsibility First Conference on Computers, Freedom, and Privacy*, Burlingame, CA, March 28, 1991. https://archive.md/yF4Z3.

Golianopoulos, Thomas. 2010. "The Original WikiLeaker." *The New York Observer*, December 8, 2010. https://archive.md/xY4VZ and https://archive.md/hNoZk.

Grabowski, Mark. 2019. *Cryptocurrencies: A Primer on Digital Money.* New York: Routledge.

Grima, Joseph. 2011. "Open Source Design 01: The Architects of Information." *Domus 948*, June 2011. https://archive.md/mXO8o.

Greenberg, Andy. 2012. *This Machine Kills Secrets: How WikiLeakers, Cypherpunks, and Hacktivists Aim to Free the World's Information.* New York: Dutton.

Greenberg, Andy. 2013. "Collected Quotations of the Dread Pirate Roberts, Founder of Underground Drug Site Silk Road And Radical Libertarian." *Forbes*, April 29, 2013. https://archive.md/whWOv.

Greenwald, Glenn. 2011. "WikiLeaks cables and the Iraq War." *Salon*, October 23, 2011. https://archive.md/pzF19.

Greenwald, Glenn. 2014. *No Place to Hide: Edward Snowden, the NSA, and the U.S. Surveillance State.* New York: Picador.

Greenwald, Glenn. 2017. "Gina Haspel, Trump's Pick for CIA Director, Ran a Black Site for Torture." *The Intercept*, February 2, 2017. https://archive.md/3ppKB.

Greenwald, Glenn. 2021. "Julian Assange Loses Appeal: British High Court Accepts U.S. Request to Extradite Him for Trial." *Glenn Greenwald* (blog), December 10, 2021. https://archive.md/Yayxu.

Gürses, Seda, Arun Kundnani, and Joris Van Hoboken. 2016. "Crypto and Empire: The Contradictions of Counter-Surveillance Advocacy." *Media, Culture & Society* 38, no. 4: 576–590.

Hafner, Katie, and John Markoff. 1995. *Cyberpunk: Outlaws and Hackers on the Computer Frontier.* New York: Touchstone.

Handley, Robert L., and Lou Rutigliano. 2012. "Journalistic Field Wars: Defending and Attacking the National Narrative in a Diversifying Journalistic Field." *Media, Culture & Society* 34, no. 6: 744–760.

Harrison, Sarah. 2015. "Indexing the Empire." In *The WikiLeaks Files*, 145–158. New York: Verso.

Hayase, Nozomi. 2016. "WikiLeaks, 10 Years of Pushing the Boundaries of Free Speech." *Common Dreams*, October 4, 2016. https://archive.fo/GRn4u.

Hellegren, Z. Isadora. 2017. "A History of Crypto-Discourse: Encryption as a Site of Struggles to Define Internet Freedom." *Internet Histories* 1, no. 4: 285–311.

Hobbes, Thomas. 1994. *Leviathan, with selected variants from the Latin edition of 1668.* Edited by Edwin Curley. Indianapolis: Hackett Publishing Company.

Holden, Joshua. 2017. *The Mathematics of Secrets: Cryptography from Caesar Ciphers to Digital Encryption*. Princeton, NJ: Princeton University Press.

Hsieh, Steven. 2013. "Why Did the Justice System Target Aaron Swartz?" *Rolling Stone*, January 23, 2013. https://archive.md/qBF5W.

Hughes, Eric. 2001. "A Cypherpunk's Manifesto." In *Crypto Anarchy, Cyberstates, and Pirate Utopias*, edited by Peter Ludlow, 81–83. Cambridge: MIT Press.

Illich, Ivan. 2009. *Tools for Conviviality*. New York: Marion Boyars.

Innis, Harold A. 2007. *Empire and Communications*. Lanham, MD: Rowman & Littlefield.

Innis, Harold A. 2008. *The Bias of Communication*. Second Edition. Toronto: University of Toronto Press.

Jarvis, Craig. 2021. *Crypto Wars: The Fight for Privacy in the Digital Age: A Political History of Digital Encryption*. Boca Raton, FL: CRC Press.

Kahn, David. 1967. *The Codebreakers: The Story of Secret Writing*. New York: Macmillan.

Khatchadourian, Raffi. 2010. "No Secrets: Julian Assange's Mission for Total Transparency." *New Yorker*, June 7, 2010. http://archive.fo/nspvA.

Lee, Timothy B. 2013. "The Inside Story of Aaron Swartz's Campaign to Liberate Court Filings." *Ars Technica*, February 8, 2013. https://archive.md/VXuSS.

Levy, Steve. 2001. *Crypto: How the Code Rebels Beat the Government—Saving Privacy in the Digital Age*. New York: Penguin.

Levy, Steve. 2010. *Hackers: Heroes of the Computer Revolution—25th Anniversary Edition*. Cambridge: O'Reilly Media, Inc.

"Link Encryption vs. End-to-End Encryption." 2009. *Logical Security* (blog), December 29, 2009. https://archive.md/o2SpF.

Locke, John. 1980. *Second Treatise of Government*. Edited by C. B. Macpherson. Indianapolis: Hackett Publishing Company.

Lynch, Lisa. 2012. "'That's Not Leaking, It's Pure Editorial': Wikileaks, Scientific Journalism, and Journalistic Expertise." *Canadian Journal of Media Studies* (Fall): 40–69.

Lynch, Lisa. 2013. "The Leak Heard Round the World? Cablegate in the Evolving Global Mediascape." In *Beyond WikiLeaks: Implications for the Future of Communications, Journalism and Society*, edited by Benedetta Brevini, Arne Hintz, and Patrick McCurdy, 56–77. New York: Palgrave Macmillan.

Manne, Robert. 2011. "The Cypherpunk Revolutionary." *The Monthly*, February 16, 2011. http://archive.fo/kwI60.

Marechal, Natalie. 2013. "WikiLeaks and the Public Sphere: Dissent and Control in Cyberworld." *The International Journal of Technology, Knowledge, and Society* 9: 93–106.

Martin, Keith. 2020. *Cryptography: The Key to Digital Security, How It Works, and Why it Matters*. New York: W. W. Norton.

May, Timothy C. 1996a. "Introduction to BlackNet." In *High Noon on the Electronic Frontier: Conceptual Issues in Cyberspace*, edited by Peter Ludlow, 241–243. Cambridge: The MIT Press.

May, Timothy C. 1996b. "BlackNet Worries." In *High Noon on the Electronic Frontier: Conceptual Issues in Cyberspace*, edited by Peter Ludlow, 245–249. Cambridge: The MIT Press.

May, Timothy C. 2001a. "True Nyms and Crypto Anarchy." In *True Names and the Opening of Cyberspace*, edited by James Frenkel, 33–86. New York: TOR Books.

May, Timothy C. 2001b. "A Crypto Anarchist Manifesto." In *Crypto Anarchy, Cyberstates, and Pirate Utopias*, edited by Peter Ludlow, 61–63. Cambridge: MIT Press.

May, Timothy C. 2001c. "Crypto Anarchy and Virtual Communities." In *Crypto Anarchy, Cyberstates, and Pirate Utopias*, edited by Peter Ludlow, 65–79. Cambridge: MIT Press.

May, Timothy C. 2018. "Enough with the ICO-Me-So-Horny-Get-Rich-Quick-Lambo Crypto." *Coindesk*, October 19, 2018. https://archive.md/zojKA.

McShea, Robert J. 1979. "Human Nature Ethical Theory." *Philosophy and Phenomenological Research* 39, no. 3: 386–401.

Melzer, Nils. 2019. "Demasking the Torture of Julian Assange." *Medium* (blog), June 26, 2019. https://archive.md/nigOm.

Michaud, Thomas. 2008. "Science Fiction and Politics: Cyberpunk Science Fiction as Political Philosophy." In *New Boundaries in Political Science Fiction*, edited by Donald M. Hassler and Clyde Wilcox, 65–77. Columbia: The University of South Carolina Press.

Milan, Stefania, and Lonneke van der Velden. 2016. "The Alternative Epistemologies of Data Activism." *Digital Culture and Society* 2, no. 2: 57–74.

Mill, John Stuart. 1873. *Considerations on Representative Government*. New York: Harper & Brothers.

Milburn, Colin. 2020. "Activism." In *The Routledge Companion to Cyberpunk Culture*, edited by Anna McFarlane, Lars Schmeink, and Graham Murphy, 373–381. New York: Routledge.

Mitcham, Carl. 1994. *Thinking through Technology: The Path between Engineering and Philosophy*. Chicago: University of Chicago Press.

Mitchell, Greg. 2008. *So Wrong for So Long: How the Press, the Pundits—and the President—Failed on Iraq*. New York: Union Square Press.

Monsees, Linda. 2020. *Crypto-Politics: Encryption and Democratic Practices in the Digital Era*. New York: Routledge.

Moore, Adam. 2011. "Privacy, Security, and Government Surveillance: WikiLeaks and the New Accountability." *Public Affairs Quarterly* 25, no. 2: 141–156.

Nakamoto, Satoshi. 2008. "Bitcoin: A Peer-to-Peer Electronic Cash System." October 31, 2008. https://bitcoin.org/bitcoin.pdf.

Narayanan, Arvind. 2013a. "What Happened to the Crypto Dream?, Part 1." *IEEE Security & Privacy* 11, no. 2: 75–76.

Narayanan, Arvind. 2013b. "What Happened to the Crypto Dream?, Part 2." *IEEE Security & Privacy* 11, no. 3: 68–71.

Nozick, Robert. 1974. *Anarchy, State, and Utopia.* New York: Basic Books.
O'Day, John C. 2019. "Corporate Media Have Second Thoughts about Exiling Julian Assange from Journalism." *Fairness & Accuracy in Reporting,* June 5, 2019. http://archive.fo/ry6Ik.
Peters, John Durham. 1999. *Speaking into the Air: A History of the Idea of Communication.* Chicago: University of Chicago Press.
"Philosophy of the GNU Project." n.d. Free Software Foundation, Inc. https://archive.md/WLFz6.
Pope-Weidemann, Marienna. 2013. "Review of *Cypherpunks: Freedom and the Future of the Internet.*" *Counterfire,* September 13, 2013. https://archive.md/Oyczc.
Prathap, Madana. 2021. "Bitcoin Does Not Make Payments Anonymous—Just Really Hard to Trace." *Business Insider India,* August 5, 2021. https://archive.md/AqYLh.
"Proprietary Software Is Often Malware." 2021. Free Software Foundation, Inc. https://archive.md/uxhz3.
Repko, Allen. 2008. *Interdisciplinary Research: Process and Theory.* Thousand Oaks, CA: Sage Publications.
Rexhepi, Piro. 2016. "Liberal Luxury: Decentering Snowden, Surveillance, and Privilege." *Big Data & Society* (July–December): 1–3.
Rid, Thomas. 2016. *Rise of the Machines: A Cybernetic History.* New York: W. W. Norton.
Rivest, Ron, Adi Shamir, and Leonard Adleman. 1978. "A Method for Obtaining Digital Signatures and Public-Key Cryptosystems." *Communications of the ACM* 21, no. 2: 120–126.
Rogaway, Phillip. 2015. "The Moral Character of Cryptographic Work." Cryptology ePrint Archive, Report 2015/1162. https://ia.cr/2015/1162.
Rosen, Armin. 2014. "A Radical Pro-Transparency Website Is Raising Money to Annoy Glenn Greenwald." *Business Insider,* May 30, 2014. https://archive.md/UWSCK.
Rousseau, Jean-Jacques. 1987. *Basic Political Writings.* Translated and edited by Donald A. Cress. Indianapolis: Hackett Publishing Company.
Rubenfeld, Jed. 2008. "The End of Privacy." *Stanford Law Review* 61: 101–161.
Schmidt, Michael. 2013. "Ex-C.I.A. Officer Sentenced to 30 Months in Leak." *New York Times,* January 25, 2013. https://archive.md/r0IDu
Schneier, Bruce. 1996. *Applied Cryptography.* Second Edition. New York: John Wiley & Sons, Inc.
Shane, Scott. 2010. "Keeping Secrets WikiSafe." *The New York Times,* December 11, 2010. https://archive.fo/Ah54H.
Singh, Simon. 2000. *The Code Book: The Science of Secrecy from Ancient Egypt to Quantum Cryptography.* New York: Anchor Books.
Stallman, Richard. 2005. "Bill Gates and Other Communists." Free Software Foundation, Inc. https://archive.md/6L2x9.
Stallman, Richard. 2021. "Why Open Source Misses the Point of Free Software." Free Software Foundation, Inc. https://archive.md/Y1E2k.

Sterling, Bruce. 1986. Preface to *Burning Chrome*, xi–xiv. Written by William Gibson. New York: Harper Collins.

Sterling, Bruce. 1992. *The Hacker Crackdown: Law and Disorder on the Electronic Frontier.* New York: Bantam Books.

Sterling, Bruce. 2010. "The Blast Shack." *Webstock*, December 22, 2010. https://archive.md/eZFZC.

Suber, Peter. 2015. "Open Access Overview." December 5, 2015. https://archive.ph/OFwDw.

Swartz, Aaron. 2008. "Guerilla Open Access Manifesto." July 2008. https://archive.org/stream/GuerillaOpenAccessManifesto/Goamjuly2008_djvu.txt.

Taylor, Sven. 2017. "VPNs are Lying about Logs." *Restore Privacy* (blog), October 8, 2017. https://archive.md/w9Usl.

Turner, Fred. 2006. *From Counterculture to Cyberculture: Stewart Brand, the Whole Earth Network, and the Rise of Digital Utopianism.* Chicago, IL: University of Chicago Press.

"UN expert says 'Collective Persecution' of Julian Assange Must End Now." 2019. United Nations Office of the High Commissioner for Human Rights. May 31, 2019. https://archive.fo/xZ2Zq.

van der Vlist, Fernando N. 2017. "Counter-Mapping Surveillance: A Critical Cartography of Mass Surveillance Technology After Snowden." *Surveillance & Society* 15, no. 1: 137–157.

Van Hoboken, Joris V. J. 2014. "Privacy and Security in the Cloud: Some Realism about Technical Solutions to Transnational Surveillance in the Post-Snowden Era." *Maine Law Review* 66, no. 2: 487–534.

Villena Saldaña, David. 2011. "Julian Assange: periodismo, científico, conspiración y ética hacker." *Quehacer* 181: 58–69.

Vine, David. 2015. *Base Nation: How U.S. Military Bases Abroad Harm America and the World.* New York: Metropolitan Books.

Webster, Frank. 2006. *Theories of the Information Society.* Third Edition. New York: Routledge.

Wiener, Norbert. 1961. *Cybernetics: Or Control and Communication in the Animal and the Machine.* Second Edition. Cambridge: MIT Press.

"WikiLeaks founder Julian Assange on the 'War Logs': 'I Enjoy Crushing Bastards.'" 2010. *Spiegel*, July 26, 2010. https://archive.fo/yLNN.

Zuboff, Shoshana. 2019. *The Age of Surveillance Capitalism: The Fight for a Human Future at the New Frontier of Power.* New York: Public Affairs.

Index

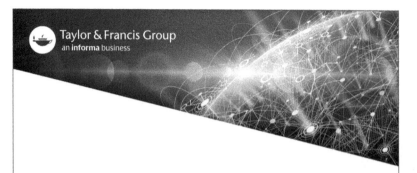